what's cooking

One Pot

what's cooking
One Pot

A collection of must-have recipes for all occasions

First published in 2010
LOVE FOOD is an imprint of Parragon Books Ltd

Parragon
Queen Street House
4 Queen Street
Bath BA1 1HE, UK

ISBN: 978-1-4454-0321-2

Printed in Indonesia

Cover design by Talking Design
Cover image by Clive Streeter
Internal design by Simon Levy
Additional photography by Mike Cooper
Food styling by Sumi Glass and Lincoln Jefferson
Introduction by Christine McFadden

Notes for the Reader

This book uses imperial, metric, and US cup measurements. Follow the same units of measurement throughout; do not mix imperial and metric. All spoon measurements are level: teaspoons are assumed to be 5 ml, and tablespoons are assumed to be 15 ml. Unless otherwise stated, milk is assumed to be whole, eggs and individual vegetables such as potatoes are medium, and pepper is freshly ground black pepper.

The times given are an approximate guide only. Preparation times differ according to the techniques used by different people and the cooking times may also vary from those given as a result of the type of oven used. Optional ingredients, variations or serving suggestions have not been included in the calculations.

Recipes using raw or very lightly cooked eggs should be avoided by infants, the elderly, pregnant women, convalescents, and anyone with a chronic condition. Pregnant and breastfeeding women are advised to avoid eating peanuts and peanut products. Sufferers from nut allergies should be aware that some of the ready-prepared ingredients used in the recipes in this book may contain nuts. Always check the packaging before use.

CONTENTS

INTRODUCTION

These days most of us lead action-packed lives, either at work or as a busy parent, or both. Time-consuming meal preparation, let alone clearing up afterward, just doesn't fit in very easily. Yet most of us care about health and want to eat nutritious home-cooked food. What could be more satisfying than something simmering on the stove, filling the air with delicious aromas?

If you love cooking but are short of time, then *What's Cooking One Pot* will be a lifesaver. As the name suggests, all the dishes can be cooked in a single pot with other ingredients, leaving you with very little to wash up but plenty of time to get on with other things.

The one-pot method is a relaxed and flexible way of cooking, easily adjusted to whatever ingredients you have in your refrigerator or pantry. If one ingredient is missing, it's usually possible to substitute another. If you're short of space or equipment, one-pot cooking is ideal—you need just one pot and a single burner.

One-pot cooking doesn't limit you to soups and stews, though this book contains plenty of recipes for these. In many parts of the world, cooking in a single pot is the norm, whether it's a cauldron, a wok, a tagine, or a bean pot. Many dishes grew up out of necessity when food and fuel were scarce. Others were created for religious reasons—the Muslim Ramadan, for example, or the Jewish Sabbath when orthodox believers are forbidden to work or cook. The pot could be left to simmer slowly overnight ready to serve at sunset the following day. In cold climates, it was the conviviality and friendship of communal eating that inspired many one-pot dishes. Think of Swiss fondue, Hungarian goulash, or Mongolian hot pot.

As the recipes in the book demonstrate, this no-frills way of cooking is the ultimate in convenience since everything is ready at the same time. It's the ideal food for solitary suppers or for feeding a crowd. Just put the pot on the table and tuck in.

GETTING STARTED

Although one-pot cooking appears simple, it relies on a certain amount of preplanning to ensure that things go smoothly. More importantly, getting organized from the start means you can relax and enjoy the actual process of cooking instead of running around the kitchen looking for missing utensils or, worse still, discovering too late that you've run out of a vital ingredient.

Before you start to cook:

- Read the recipe all the way through, then plan the sequence according to what needs soaking, chopping, precooking, and so on.
- Have the right tools and cookware at hand
- Make sure knives are sharp
- Wash fresh vegetables, fruits, and herbs
- Assemble all the ingredients then measure or weigh them as necessary
- Complete any preparation beforehand, such as chopping or grating
- Have the prepared ingredients lined up in bowls, ready to add to the pot at the correct time
- Clear up as you go along

USEFUL UTENSILS

As well as basics such as knives and cutting boards, there are a number of additional utensils that make one-pot cooking easier and safer.

Though you can happily leave the pot to simmer while you get on with something else, it's still important to keep track of temperature and time. Thermometers are essential for food safety, and a timer with a loud ring is invaluable for reminding you when the dish needs your attention. You'll also need spoons and spatulas for stirring, and tools for turning and lifting ingredients that are precooked in stages before they go into the pot. A sturdy long-handled fork or multipronged meat lifter are handy for large pieces of meat, while stainless steel spring-action tongs let you clasp smaller pieces of food securely. A perforated shallow skimmer is useful for removing froth and foam from the surface of stews.

Although one-pot recipes are infinitely flexible, it's worth investing in proper measuring spoons and cups, as well as a kitchen scale, especially if you are new to cooking. Once you gain experience and confidence, it's fine to add a pinch of this and a handful of that.

The joy of one-pot meals is that they can be brought straight from oven to table. However, heat can damage unprotected surfaces, so it's a good idea to have a trivet or pot stand at the ready.

COOKWARE

For most of the recipes in this book, a few heavy-bottom saucepans and casseroles in varying sizes with tight-fitting lids make up the basic equipment. You'll also need a high-sided skillet, a wok, good-quality roasting pans that won't warp or twist, and some shallow baking dishes for gratins and crumbles.

FRESH PRODUCE

Wholesome fresh vegetables, meat, poultry, and fish add valuable nutrients to one-pot meals, as well as color, texture, and appetizing flavors.

Vegetables

Vegetables are one of the most important sources of vitamins, minerals, and fiber. They are packed with carotenoids (the plant form of vitamin A), vitamin C, and vitamin E, which collectively protect against heart disease and some cancers.

Meat and poultry

Meat and poultry provide high-quality protein, important minerals such as iron and zinc, and B vitamins, which are needed to release energy from food. Meat tends to be high in fat, so if you're trying to cut down, trim off any excess or choose lean cuts.

Fish and seafood

Dense-fleshed fish and seafood make marvelous one-pot meals. They provide protein and essential minerals, while oily fish such as tuna are a unique source of omega-3 fatty acids that protect against heart disease and feed the brain.

Fresh herbs

A generous sprinkling of fresh herbs added at the end of cooking will provide delightful fragrance and color to one pot meals.

PANTRY ITEMS

A pantry judiciously stocked with a few essentials means you are never without the makings of a one-pot meal.

Grains

Grains such as rice, barley, oats, quinoa, and bulgur wheat contain a range of concentrated nutrients. Perked up with colorful spices and herbs, they form a nutritious base to which meat, fish, and vegetables can be added as necessary.

Beans

Dried beans are packed with nutrients, and provide a mellow background to more strongly flavored ingredients. Canned beans are invaluable since you can add them to the pot without soaking or precooking.

Pasta

Short pasta shapes, from tiny star shapes to coils and fat tubes, make the basis for endless one pot meals. Pasta shapes can be precooked or added to the pot with plenty of liquid.

Seeds and nuts

Crunchy seeds and nuts provide texture and, if chopped finely, can give body to the cooking liquid. Pumpkin, sunflower, and sesame seeds are particularly nutritious, as are walnuts, almonds, and Brazil nuts.

Sauces and pastes

A judicious splash of sauce or dollop of paste can perk up an otherwise bland dish. Soy sauce, Worcestershire sauce, and Tabasco all have outstanding flavors, as do tomato paste, tapenade, and mustards. Ready-made jars of ethnic sauces also add exciting flavors, and save time too.

Spices and dried herbs

For the best flavor, buy spices whole (including pepper) and grind them as needed. Rosemary, thyme, and oregano are the best herbs to use dried; the more delicate varieties are better when fresh. Add spices and dried herbs at the early stages of cooking to bring out the full flavor.

SOUPS

CHUNKY VEGETABLE SOUP

Put the carrots, onion, garlic, potatoes, celery, mushrooms, tomatoes, and stock into a large pan. Stir in the bay leaf and herbs. Bring to a boil, then reduce the heat, cover, and let simmer for 25 minutes.

Add the corn and cabbage and return to a boil. Reduce the heat, cover, and simmer for 5 minutes, or until the vegetables are tender. Remove and discard the bay leaf. Season to taste with pepper.

Ladle into warmed bowls and serve at once with crusty bread rolls.

SERVES 6

2 carrots, sliced

1 onion, diced

1 garlic clove, crushed

12 oz/350 g new potatoes, diced

2 celery stalks, sliced

4 oz/115 g button mushrooms, quartered

14 oz/400 g canned chopped tomatoes in tomato juice

2½ cups vegetable stock

1 bay leaf

1 tsp dried mixed herbs or 1 tbsp chopped fresh mixed herbs

½ cup corn kernels, frozen or canned, drained

2 oz/55 g green cabbage, shredded

pepper

crusty whole wheat or white bread rolls, to serve

MINESTRONE

Heat the oil in a large pan. Add the garlic, onions, and prosciutto and cook over medium heat, stirring, for 3 minutes, until slightly softened. Add the red and orange bell peppers and the chopped tomatoes and cook for another 2 minutes, stirring. Stir in the stock, then add the celery, beans, cabbage, peas, and parsley. Season with salt and pepper. Bring to a boil, then lower the heat and simmer for 30 minutes.

Add the vermicelli to the pan. Cook for another 10–12 minutes, or according to the instructions on the package. Remove from the heat and ladle into serving bowls. Garnish with freshly grated Parmesan, to serve.

SERVES 4

2 tbsp olive oil

2 garlic cloves, chopped

2 red onions, chopped

2¾ oz/75 g prosciutto, sliced

1 red bell pepper, seeded and chopped

1 orange bell pepper, seeded and chopped

14 oz/400 g canned chopped tomatoes

4 cups vegetable stock

1 celery stalk, trimmed and sliced

14 oz/400 g canned borlotti beans, drained

3½ oz/100 g green leafy cabbage, shredded

2¾ oz/75 g frozen peas, thawed

1 tbsp chopped fresh parsley

2¾ oz/75 g dried vermicelli

salt and pepper

freshly grated Parmesan cheese, to garnish

FRENCH ONION SOUP

Heat the olive oil in a large, heavy-bottom pan, then add the onions and cook, stirring occasionally, for 10 minutes, until they are just beginning to brown. Stir in the chopped garlic, sugar, and thyme, then reduce the heat and cook, stirring occasionally, for 30 minutes, or until the onions are golden brown.

Sprinkle in the flour and cook, stirring, for 1–2 minutes. Stir in the wine. Gradually stir in the stock and bring to a boil, skimming off any foam that rises to the surface, then reduce the heat and simmer for 45 minutes. Meanwhile, toast the bread on both sides under a preheated medium broiler. Rub the toast with the whole garlic clove.

Ladle the soup into 6 flameproof bowls set on a baking sheet. Float a piece of toast in each bowl and divide the grated cheese among them. Place under a preheated medium–hot broiler for 2–3 minutes, or until the cheese has just melted. Garnish with thyme sprigs and serve.

SERVES 6

3 tbsp olive oil

1 lb 8 oz/675 g onions, thinly sliced

4 garlic cloves, 3 chopped and 1 peeled but kept whole

1 tsp sugar

2 tsp chopped fresh thyme

2 tbsp all-purpose flour

½ cup dry white wine

8 cups vegetable stock

6 slices of French bread

3 cups grated Swiss cheese

fresh thyme sprigs, to garnish

BEEF GOULASH SOUP

Heat the oil in a large, wide saucepan over medium–high heat. Add the beef and sprinkle with salt and pepper. Cook until lightly browned.

Reduce the heat and add the onions and garlic. Cook for about 3 minutes, stirring frequently, until the onions are softened. Stir in the flour and continue cooking for 1 minute.

Gradually stir in the water and combine well, scraping the bottom of the pan to mix in the flour. Stir in the tomatoes, carrot, pepper, paprika, caraway seeds, oregano, and stock.

Bring just to a boil. Reduce the heat, cover, and simmer gently for about 40 minutes, stirring occasionally, until all the vegetables are tender.

Add the tagliatelle to the soup and simmer for an additional 20 minutes, or until the tagliatelle is cooked.

Taste the soup and adjust the seasoning, if necessary. Ladle into warmed bowls and top each with a tablespoonful of sour cream. Garnish with cilantro and serve.

SERVES 6

1 tbsp olive oil

1 lb 2 oz/500 g fresh lean ground beef

2 onions, finely chopped

2 garlic cloves, finely chopped

2 tbsp all-purpose flour

1 cup water

14 oz/400 g canned chopped tomatoes

1 carrot, finely chopped

8 oz/225 g red bell pepper, roasted, peeled, seeded, and chopped

1 tsp Hungarian paprika

¼ tsp caraway seeds

pinch of dried oregano

4 cups beef stock

2 oz/55 g tagliatelle, broken into small pieces

salt and pepper

sour cream and sprigs of fresh cilantro, to garnish

BACON & LENTIL SOUP

Heat a large, heavy-bottom saucepan or flameproof casserole. Add the bacon and cook over medium heat, stirring, for 4–5 minutes, or until the fat runs. Add the chopped onion, carrots, celery, turnip, and potato and cook, stirring frequently, for 5 minutes.

Add the lentils and bouquet garni and pour in the stock. Bring to a boil, reduce the heat, and simmer for 1 hour, or until the lentils are tender.

Remove and discard the bouquet garni and season the soup to taste with pepper, and with salt if necessary. Ladle into warmed soup bowls and serve.

SERVES 4

1 lb/450 g thick, rindless smoked bacon strips, diced

1 onion, chopped

2 carrots, sliced

2 celery stalks, chopped

1 turnip, chopped

1 large potato, chopped

generous 2¼ cups Puy lentils

1 bouquet garni

4 cups chicken stock

salt and pepper

ASIAN
LAMB SOUP

Trim all visible fat from the lamb and slice the meat thinly. Cut the slices into bite-size pieces. Spread the meat in one layer on a plate and sprinkle over the garlic and 1 tablespoon of the soy sauce. Marinate, covered, for at least 10 minutes or up to 1 hour.

Put the stock in a saucepan with the ginger, lemongrass, remaining soy sauce, and the chili paste. Bring just to a boil, reduce the heat, cover, and simmer for 10–15 minutes.

When ready to serve the soup, drop the tomatoes, scallions, bean sprouts, and cilantro leaves into the stock.

Heat the oil in a skillet and add the lamb with its marinade. Stir-fry the lamb just until it is no longer red and divide among the warmed bowls.

Ladle over the hot stock and serve immediately.

SERVES 4

5½ oz/150 g lean tender lamb, such as neck fillet or leg steak

2 garlic cloves, very finely chopped

2 tbsp soy sauce

5 cups chicken stock

1 tbsp grated fresh ginger

2-inch/5-cm piece lemongrass, sliced into very thin rounds

¼ tsp chili paste, or to taste

6–8 cherry tomatoes, quartered

4 scallions, finely sliced

1¾ oz/50 g bean sprouts, snapped in half

2 tbsp cilantro leaves

1 tsp olive oil

CREAM OF CHICKEN SOUP

Melt the butter in a large pan over medium heat. Add the shallots and cook, stirring, for 3 minutes, until slightly softened. Add the leek and cook for another 5 minutes, stirring. Add the chicken, stock, and herbs, and season with salt and pepper. Bring to a boil, then lower the heat and simmer for 25 minutes, until the chicken is tender and cooked through. Remove from the heat and cool for 10 minutes.

Transfer the soup into a food processor or blender and process until smooth (you may need to do this in batches). Return the soup to the rinsed-out pan and warm over low heat for 5 minutes.

Stir in the cream and cook for another 2 minutes, then remove from the heat and ladle into serving bowls. Garnish with sprigs of thyme and serve immediately.

SERVES 4

3 tbsp butter

4 shallots, chopped

1 leek, sliced

1 lb/450 g skinless chicken breasts, chopped

2½ cups chicken stock

1 tbsp chopped fresh parsley

1 tbsp chopped fresh thyme, plus extra sprigs to garnish

¾ cup heavy cream

salt and pepper

CHICKEN & LEEK SOUP

Heat the oil in a large pan over medium heat, add the onions, carrots, and the 2 coarsely chopped leeks, and cook for 3–4 minutes until just golden brown.

Wipe the chicken inside and out and remove and discard any excess skin and fat.

Put the chicken into the pan with the cooked vegetables and add the bay leaves. Pour in enough cold water just to cover and season well with salt and pepper. Bring to a boil, then reduce the heat, cover, and simmer for 1–1½ hours. Skim off any foam that forms from time to time.

Remove the chicken from the stock, remove and discard the skin, then remove all the meat. Cut the meat into neat pieces.

Strain the stock through a colander, discard the vegetables and bay leaves, and return to the rinsed-out pan. Expect to have 4–5 cups of stock. If you have time, it is a good idea to let the stock cool so that the fat solidifies and can be removed. If not, blot the fat off the surface with paper towels.

Heat the stock to simmering point, add the sliced leeks and prunes to the pan, and heat for about 1 minute.

Return the chicken to the pan and heat through. Serve immediately in warmed deep dishes, garnished with the parsley.

SERVES 6–8

2 tbsp olive oil

2 onions, coarsely chopped

2 carrots, coarsely chopped

5 leeks, 2 coarsely chopped,
   3 thinly sliced

1 chicken, weighing 3 lb/1.3 kg

2 bay leaves

6 prunes, pitted and sliced

salt and pepper

sprigs of fresh parsley, to garnish

THAI CHICKEN-COCONUT SOUP

Put the dried noodles in a large bowl with enough lukewarm water to cover and soak for 20 minutes, until soft. Alternatively, cook according to the package instructions. Drain well and set aside.

Meanwhile, bring the stock to a boil in a large pan over high heat. Lower the heat, add the lemongrass, ginger, lime leaves, and chile, and simmer for 5 minutes. Add the chicken and continue simmering for an additional 3 minutes, or until cooked. Stir in the coconut cream, nam pla, and lime juice, and continue simmering for 3 minutes. Add the bean sprouts and scallions and simmer for an additional 1 minute. Taste and gradually add extra nam pla or lime juice at this point, if needed. Remove and discard the lemongrass stalk.

Divide the noodles among 4 bowls. Bring the soup back to a boil, then ladle into the bowls. The heat of the soup will warm the noodles. To garnish, sprinkle with cilantro leaves.

SERVES 4

4 oz/115 g dried cellophane noodles

5 cups chicken stock or vegetable stock

1 lemongrass stalk, crushed

½-inch/1-cm piece fresh ginger, peeled and very finely chopped

2 fresh kaffir lime leaves, thinly sliced

1 fresh red chile, or to taste, seeded and thinly sliced

2 skinless, boneless chicken breasts, thinly sliced

scant 1 cup coconut cream

about 2 tbsp nam pla (Thai fish sauce)

about 1 tbsp fresh lime juice

scant ½ cup bean sprouts

4 scallions, green parts only, finely sliced

fresh cilantro leaves, to garnish

TURKEY & LENTIL SOUP

Heat the oil in a large pan. Add the garlic and onion and cook over medium heat, stirring, for 3 minutes, until slightly softened. Add the mushrooms, bell pepper, and tomatoes, and cook for another 5 minutes, stirring. Pour in the stock and red wine, then add the cauliflower, carrot, and red lentils. Season to taste with salt and pepper. Bring to a boil, then lower the heat and simmer for 25 minutes, until the vegetables are tender and cooked through.

Add the turkey and zucchini to the pan and cook for 10 minutes. Stir in the shredded basil and cook for another 5 minutes, then remove from the heat and ladle into serving bowls. Garnish with fresh basil sprigs and serve immediately.

SERVES 4

1 tbsp olive oil

1 garlic clove, chopped

1 large onion, chopped

7 oz/200 g white mushrooms, sliced

1 red bell pepper, seeded and chopped

6 tomatoes, skinned, seeded, and chopped

4 cups chicken stock

²⁄₃ cup red wine

3 oz/85 g cauliflower florets

1 carrot, chopped

1 cup red lentils

12 oz/350 g cooked turkey, chopped

1 zucchini, chopped

1 tbsp shredded fresh basil

salt and pepper

sprigs of fresh basil, to garnish

DUCK WITH SCALLION SOUP

Slash the skin of the duck 3 or 4 times with a sharp knife and rub in the curry paste. Cook the duck breasts, skin-side down, in a wok or skillet over high heat for 2–3 minutes. Turn over, reduce the heat, and cook for an additional 3–4 minutes, until cooked through. Lift out and slice thickly. Set aside and keep warm.

Meanwhile, heat the oil in a wok or large skillet and stir-fry half the scallions with the garlic, ginger, carrots, and red bell pepper for 2–3 minutes. Pour in the stock and add the chili sauce, soy sauce, and mushrooms. Bring to a boil, reduce the heat, and simmer for 4–5 minutes.

Ladle the soup into warmed bowls, top with the duck slices, and garnish with the remaining scallions. Serve immediately.

SERVES 2

2 duck breasts, skin on

2 tbsp red curry paste

2 tbsp vegetable oil or peanut oil

bunch of scallions, chopped

2 garlic cloves, crushed

2-inch/5-cm piece fresh ginger, grated

2 carrots, thinly sliced

1 red bell pepper, seeded and cut into strips

4 cups chicken stock

2 tbsp sweet chili sauce

3–4 tbsp Thai soy sauce

14 oz/400 g canned straw mushrooms, drained

SEAFOOD CHOWDER

Discard any mussels with broken shells or any that refuse to close when tapped. Rinse and pull off any beards. Put the mussels in a large heavy-bottom saucepan. Cover tightly and cook over high heat for about 4 minutes, or until the mussels open, shaking the pan occasionally. Discard any that remain closed. When they are cool enough to handle, remove the mussels from the shells and set aside.

Put the flour in a mixing bowl and very slowly whisk in enough of the stock to make a thick paste. Whisk in a little more stock to make a smooth liquid.

Melt the butter in a heavy-bottom saucepan over medium–low heat. Add the onion, cover, and cook for 3 minutes, stirring frequently, until it softens.

Add the remaining fish stock and bring to a boil. Slowly whisk in the flour mixture until well combined and bring back to a boil, whisking constantly. Add the mussel cooking liquid. Season with salt, if needed, and pepper. Reduce the heat and simmer, partially covered, for 15 minutes.

Add the whitefish and the mussels and continue simmering, stirring occasionally, for about 5 minutes, or until the fish is cooked and begins to flake.

Stir in the shrimp and cream. Taste and adjust the seasoning. Simmer for 2–3 minutes longer to heat through. Ladle into warmed bowls, sprinkle with dill, and serve.

SERVES 6

2 lb 4 oz/1 kg live mussels

4 tbsp all-purpose flour

6¼ cups fish stock

1 tbsp butter

1 large onion, finely chopped

12 oz/350 g skinless whitefish
    fillets, such as cod, sole,
    or haddock

7 oz/200 g cooked or raw peeled
    shrimp

1¼ cups heavy cream

salt and pepper

snipped fresh dill, to garnish

BOUILLABAISSE

Heat the oil in a large pan over medium heat. Add the garlic and onions and cook, stirring, for 3 minutes. Stir in the tomatoes, stock, wine, bay leaf, saffron, and herbs. Bring to a boil, reduce the heat, cover, and simmer for 30 minutes.

Meanwhile, soak the mussels in lightly salted water for 10 minutes. Scrub the shells under cold running water and pull off any beards. Discard any mussels with broken shells or any that refuse to close when tapped. Put the rest into a large pan with a little water, bring to a boil, and cook over high heat for 4 minutes. Remove from the heat and discard any that remain closed.

When the tomato mixture is cooked, rinse the fish fillets, pat dry, and cut into chunks. Add to the pan and simmer for 5 minutes. Add the mussels, shrimp, and scallops, and season with salt and pepper to taste. Cook for 3 minutes, until the fish is cooked through. Remove from the heat, discard the bay leaf, and ladle into serving bowls.

SERVES 4

scant ½ cup olive oil

3 garlic cloves, chopped

2 onions, chopped

2 tomatoes, seeded and chopped

2¾ cups fish stock

1¾ cups white wine

1 bay leaf

pinch of saffron threads

2 tbsp chopped fresh basil

2 tbsp chopped fresh parsley

7 oz/200 g live mussels

9 oz/250 g snapper or monkfish fillets

9 oz/250 g haddock fillets, skinned

7 oz/200 g shrimp, peeled and deveined

3½ oz/100 g scallops

salt and pepper

SALMON & LEEK SOUP

Heat the oil in a large, heavy-bottom saucepan over medium heat. Add the onion and leeks and cook for about 3 minutes until they begin to soften.

Add the potato, stock, water, and bay leaf with a large pinch of salt. Bring to a boil, reduce the heat, cover, and cook gently for about 25 minutes until the vegetables are tender. Remove the bay leaf.

Let the soup cool slightly, then transfer about half of it to a food processor or blender and process until smooth. (If using a food processor, strain off the cooking liquid and reserve. Purée half the soup solids with enough cooking liquid to moisten them, then combine with the remaining liquid.)

Return the processed soup to the saucepan and stir to blend. Reheat gently over medium–low heat.

Season the salmon with salt and pepper and add to the soup. Continue cooking for about 5 minutes, stirring occasionally, until the fish is tender and starts to break up. Stir in the cream, taste, and adjust the seasoning, adding a little lemon juice if desired. Ladle into warmed bowls, garnish with chervil or parsley, and serve.

SERVES 4

1 tbsp olive oil

1 large onion, finely chopped

3 large leeks, including green parts, thinly sliced

1 potato, finely diced

2 cups fish stock

3 cups water

1 bay leaf

10½ oz/300 g skinless salmon fillet, cut into ½-inch/1-cm cubes

⅓ cup heavy cream

fresh lemon juice (optional)

salt and pepper

sprigs of fresh chervil or parsley, to garnish

MEAT

POT ROAST
WITH POTATOES
& DILL

Preheat the oven to 275°F/140°C. Mix 2 tablespoons of the flour with the salt and pepper in a shallow dish. Dip the meat to coat. Heat the oil in a flameproof casserole and brown the meat all over. Transfer to a plate. Add half the butter to the casserole and cook the onion, celery, carrots, dill seeds, and thyme for 5 minutes. Return the meat and juices to the casserole.

Pour in the wine and enough stock to reach one-third of the way up the meat. Bring to a boil, cover, and cook in the oven for 3 hours, turning the meat every 30 minutes. After it has been cooking for 2 hours, add the potatoes and more stock if necessary.

When ready, transfer the meat and vegetables to a warmed serving dish. Strain the cooking liquid to remove any solids, then return the liquid to the casserole.

Mix the remaining butter and flour to a paste. Bring the cooking liquid to a boil. Whisk in small pieces of the flour and butter paste, whisking constantly until the sauce is smooth. Pour the sauce over the meat and vegetables. Sprinkle with the fresh dill to serve.

SERVES 6

2½ tbsp all-purpose flour

1 tsp salt

¼ tsp pepper

1 rolled brisket of beef, weighing 3 lb 8 oz/1.6 kg

2 tbsp vegetable oil

2 tbsp butter

1 onion, finely chopped

2 celery stalks, diced

2 carrots, peeled and diced

1 tsp dill seeds

1 tsp dried thyme or oregano

1½ cups red wine

⅔–1 cup beef stock

4–5 potatoes, cut into large chunks and boiled until just tender

2 tbsp chopped fresh dill, to serve

BEEF STROGANOFF

Place the dried porcini mushrooms in a bowl and cover with hot water. Let soak for 20 minutes. Meanwhile, cut the beef against the grain into ¼-inch/5-mm thick slices, then into ½-inch/1-cm long strips, and reserve.

Drain the mushrooms, reserving the soaking liquid, and chop. Strain the soaking liquid through a fine-mesh strainer or coffee filter and reserve.

Heat half the oil in a large skillet. Add the shallots and cook over low heat, stirring occasionally, for 5 minutes, or until softened. Add the dried mushrooms, reserved soaking water, and whole cremini mushrooms and cook, stirring frequently, for 10 minutes, or until almost all of the liquid has evaporated, then transfer the mixture to a plate.

Heat the remaining oil in the skillet, add the beef and cook, stirring frequently, for 4 minutes, or until browned all over. You may need to do this in batches. Return the mushroom mixture to the skillet and season to taste with salt and pepper. Place the mustard and cream in a small bowl and stir to mix, then fold into the mixture. Heat through gently, then serve with freshly cooked pasta, garnished with chives.

SERVES 4

½ oz/15 g dried porcini mushrooms

12 oz/350 g beef tenderloin

2 tbsp olive oil

4 oz/115 g shallots, sliced

6 oz/175 g cremini mushrooms

½ tsp Dijon mustard

5 tbsp heavy cream

salt and pepper

freshly cooked pasta, to serve

fresh chives, to garnish

CHILI CON CARNE

Preheat the oven to 325°F/160°C. Using a sharp knife, cut the beef into ¾-inch/2-cm cubes. Heat the vegetable oil in a large flameproof casserole and cook the beef over medium heat until well seared on all sides. Remove the beef from the casserole with a slotted spoon and set aside until ready to use.

Add the onion and garlic to the casserole and cook until lightly browned, then stir in the flour and cook for 1–2 minutes.

Stir in the tomato juice and tomatoes and bring to a boil. Return the beef to the casserole and add the chili sauce, cumin, and salt and pepper to taste. Cover and cook in the preheated oven for 1½ hours, or until the beef is almost tender.

Stir in the kidney beans, oregano, and parsley, and adjust the seasoning to taste, if necessary. Cover the casserole and return to the oven for 45 minutes. Transfer to 4 large, warmed serving plates, garnish with sprigs of fresh herbs, and serve immediately with freshly cooked rice and tortillas.

SERVES 4

1 lb 10 oz/750 g lean braising beef

2 tbsp vegetable oil

1 large onion, sliced

2–4 garlic cloves, crushed

1 tbsp all-purpose flour

generous 1¾ cups tomato juice

14 oz/400 g canned tomatoes

1–2 tbsp sweet chili sauce

1 tsp ground cumin

15 oz/425 g canned red kidney beans, drained and rinsed

½ tsp dried oregano

1–2 tbsp chopped fresh parsley

salt and pepper

sprigs of fresh herbs, to garnish

freshly cooked rice and tortillas, to serve

PEPPER POT-STYLE STEW

Trim any fat or gristle from the beef and cut the meat into 1-inch/2.5-cm chunks. Toss the beef in the flour until well coated and reserve any remaining flour.

Heat the oil in a large, heavy-bottom pan and cook the onion, garlic, chile, and celery with the cloves and allspice, stirring frequently, for 5 minutes or until softened. Add the beef and cook over high heat, stirring frequently, for 3 minutes, or until browned on all sides and seared. Sprinkle in the reserved flour and cook, stirring constantly, for 2 minutes, then remove from the heat.

Add the hot pepper sauce and gradually stir in the stock, then return to the heat and bring to a boil, stirring. Reduce the heat, then cover and simmer, stirring occasionally, for 1½ hours.

Add the squash and red bell pepper to the pan and simmer for an additional 15 minutes. Add the tomatoes and okra and simmer for an additional 15 minutes, or until the beef is tender. Serve with the wild rice.

SERVES 4

1 lb/450 g braising beef

1½ tbsp all-purpose flour

2 tbsp olive oil

1 red onion, chopped

3–4 garlic cloves, crushed

1 fresh green chile, seeded and chopped

3 celery stalks, sliced

4 whole cloves

1 tsp ground allspice

1–2 tsp hot pepper sauce, or to taste

2½ cups beef stock

8 oz/225 g seeded and peeled squash, such as acorn, cut into small chunks

1 large red bell pepper, seeded and chopped

4 tomatoes, coarsely chopped

4 oz/115 g okra, trimmed and halved

freshly cooked wild rice, to serve

BEEF IN BEER WITH HERB DUMPLINGS

Preheat the oven to 325°F/160°C. Heat the oil in a flameproof casserole. Add the onions and carrots and cook over low heat, stirring occasionally, for 5 minutes, or until the onions are softened. Meanwhile, place the flour in a plastic bag and season with salt and pepper. Add the braising beef to the bag, tie the top, and shake well to coat. Do this in batches, if necessary.

Remove the vegetables from the casserole with a slotted spoon and reserve. Add the braising beef to the casserole, in batches, and cook, stirring frequently, until browned all over. Return all the meat and the onions and carrots to the casserole and sprinkle in any remaining seasoned flour. Pour in the stout and add the sugar, bay leaves, and thyme. Bring to a boil, cover, and transfer to the preheated oven to bake for 1¾ hours.

To make the herb dumplings, sift the flour and salt into a bowl. Stir in the lard and parsley and add enough of the water to make a soft dough. Shape into small balls between the palms of your hands. Add to the casserole and return to the oven for 30 minutes. Remove and discard the bay leaves and serve, sprinkled with parsley.

SERVES 6

2 tbsp corn oil

2 large onions, thinly sliced

8 carrots, sliced

4 tbsp all-purpose flour

2 lb 12 oz/1.25 kg braising beef, cut into cubes

generous 1¾ cups stout

2 tsp brown sugar

2 bay leaves

1 tbsp chopped fresh thyme

salt and pepper

herb dumplings

generous ¾ cup self-rising flour

pinch of salt

½ cup lard, chilled and cut into small pieces

2 tbsp chopped fresh parsley, plus extra to garnish

about 4 tbsp water

PORK CHOPS WITH BELL PEPPERS & CORN

Heat the oil in a large, flameproof casserole. Add the pork chops in batches and cook over medium heat, turning occasionally, for 5 minutes, or until browned. Transfer the chops to a plate with a slotted spoon.

Add the chopped onion to the casserole and cook, stirring occasionally, for 5 minutes, or until softened. Add the garlic and bell peppers and cook, stirring occasionally, for an additional 5 minutes. Stir in the corn kernels and their juices and the parsley and season to taste.

Return the chops to the casserole, spooning the vegetable mixture over them. Cover and simmer for 30 minutes, or until tender. Serve immediately with mashed potatoes.

SERVES 4

1 tbsp corn oil

4 pork chops, trimmed of visible fat

1 onion, chopped

1 garlic clove, finely chopped

1 green bell pepper, seeded and sliced

1 red bell pepper, seeded and sliced

11½ oz/325 g canned corn kernels

1 tbsp chopped fresh parsley

salt and pepper

mashed potatoes, to serve

PAPRIKA PORK

Cut the pork into 1½-inch/4-cm cubes. Heat the oil and butter in a large pan. Add the pork and cook over medium heat, stirring, for 5 minutes, or until browned. Transfer to a plate with a slotted spoon.

Add the chopped onion to the pan and cook, stirring occasionally, for 5 minutes, or until softened. Stir in the paprika and flour and cook, stirring constantly, for 2 minutes. Gradually stir in the stock and bring to a boil, stirring constantly.

Return the pork to the pan, add the sherry and sliced mushrooms, and season to taste with salt and pepper. Cover and simmer gently for 20 minutes, or until the pork is tender. Stir in the sour cream and serve.

SERVES 4

1 lb 8 oz/675 g pork tenderloin

2 tbsp corn oil

2 tbsp butter

1 onion, chopped

1 tbsp paprika

2½ tbsp all-purpose flour

1¼ cups chicken stock,
    or 1 chicken bouillon cube
    dissolved in 1¼ cups boiling
    water

4 tbsp dry sherry

4 oz/115 g button mushrooms,
    sliced

salt and pepper

⅔ cup sour cream

SAUSAGE & BEAN CASSEROLE

Prick the sausages all over with a fork. Heat 2 tablespoons of the oil in a large, heavy-bottom skillet. Add the sausages and cook over low heat, turning frequently, for 10–15 minutes, until evenly browned and cooked through. Remove them from the skillet and keep warm. Drain off the oil and wipe out the skillet with paper towels.

Heat the remaining oil in the skillet. Add the onion, garlic, and bell pepper to the skillet and cook for 5 minutes, stirring occasionally, or until softened.

Add the tomatoes to the skillet and let the mixture simmer for about 5 minutes, stirring occasionally, or until slightly reduced and thickened.

Stir the sun-dried tomato paste, cannellini beans, and Italian sausages into the mixture in the skillet. Cook for 4–5 minutes or until the mixture is piping hot. Add 4–5 tablespoons of water if the mixture becomes too dry during cooking.

Transfer the sausage and bean casserole to serving plates and serve with mashed potatoes.

SERVES 4

8 Italian sausages

3 tbsp olive oil

1 large onion, chopped

2 garlic cloves, chopped

1 green bell pepper, seeded and sliced

8 oz/225 g fresh tomatoes, skinned and chopped, or 14 oz/400 g canned tomatoes, chopped

2 tbsp sun-dried tomato paste

14 oz/400 g can cannellini beans

mashed potatoes or rice, to serve

RED CURRY PORK WITH PEPPERS

Heat the oil in a wok or large skillet and sauté the onion and garlic for 1–2 minutes, until they are softened but not browned.

Add the pork slices and stir-fry for 2–3 minutes until browned all over. Add the bell pepper, mushrooms, and curry paste.

Dissolve the coconut in the stock and add to the wok with the soy sauce. Bring to a boil and then simmer for 4–5 minutes until the liquid has reduced and thickened.

Add the tomatoes and cilantro and cook for 1–2 minutes before serving with noodles.

SERVES 4

2 tbsp vegetable oil or peanut oil

1 onion, coarsely chopped

2 garlic cloves, chopped

1 lb/450 g pork tenderloin, thickly sliced

1 red bell pepper, seeded and cut into squares

6 oz/175 g button mushrooms, quartered

2 tbsp Thai red curry paste

4 oz/115 g block creamed coconut, chopped

1¼ cups pork stock or vegetable stock

2 tbsp Thai soy sauce

4 tomatoes, peeled, seeded, and chopped

handful of fresh cilantro, chopped

boiled noodles or rice, to serve

LAMB WITH PEARS

Preheat the oven to 325°F/160°C. Heat the olive oil in a flameproof casserole over medium heat. Add the lamb and cook, turning frequently, for 5–10 minutes, or until browned on all sides.

Arrange the pear pieces on top, then sprinkle over the ginger. Cover with the potatoes. Pour in the cider and season to taste with salt and pepper. Cover and cook in the preheated oven for 1¼ hours.

Trim the stem ends of the green beans. Remove the casserole from the oven and add the beans, then re-cover and return to the oven for an additional 30 minutes. Taste and adjust the seasoning and sprinkle with the chives. Serve immediately.

SERVES 4

1 tbsp olive oil

2 lb 4 oz/1 kg best end-of-neck lamb cutlets, trimmed of visible fat

6 pears, peeled, cored, and cut into quarters

1 tsp ground ginger

4 potatoes, diced

4 tbsp hard cider

1 lb/450 g green beans

2 tbsp snipped fresh chives, to garnish

salt and pepper

CINNAMON LAMB CASSEROLE

Season the flour with salt and pepper to taste and put it with the lamb in a plastic bag, then hold the top closed and shake until the lamb cubes are lightly coated all over. Remove the lamb from the bag, then shake off any excess flour and set aside.

Heat the oil in a large, flameproof casserole and cook the onions and garlic, stirring frequently, for 5 minutes, or until softened. Add the lamb and cook over high heat, stirring frequently, for 5 minutes, or until browned on all sides and seared.

Stir the wine, vinegar, and tomatoes and their juice into the casserole, scraping any sediment from the bottom of the casserole, and bring to a boil. Reduce the heat and add the raisins, cinnamon, sugar, and bay leaf. Season to taste with salt and pepper. Cover and simmer gently for 2 hours, or until the lamb is tender.

Meanwhile, make the topping. Put the yogurt into a small serving bowl, then stir in the garlic and season to taste with salt and pepper. Cover and chill in the refrigerator until ready to serve.

Discard the bay leaf and serve the lamb hot, topped with a spoonful of the garlic yogurt, and dusted with paprika.

SERVES 6

2 tbsp all-purpose flour

2 lb 4 oz/1 kg lean boneless lamb, cubed

2 tbsp olive oil

2 large onions, sliced

1 garlic clove, finely chopped

1¼ cups full-bodied red wine

2 tbsp red wine vinegar

14 oz/400 g canned chopped tomatoes

generous ⅓ cup seedless raisins

1 tbsp ground cinnamon

pinch of sugar

1 bay leaf

salt and pepper

paprika, to garnish

topping

⅔ cup plain yogurt

2 garlic cloves, crushed

salt and pepper

LAMB STEW
WITH
CHICKPEAS

Heat 4 tablespoons of the oil in a large, heavy-bottom flameproof casserole over medium-high heat. Reduce the heat, add the chorizo, and cook for 1 minute; set aside. Add the onions to the casserole and cook for 2 minutes, then add the garlic and continue cooking for 3 minutes, or until the onions are soft, but not brown. Remove from the casserole and set aside.

Heat the remaining 2 tablespoons of oil in the casserole. Add the lamb chunks in a single layer without overcrowding the casserole, and cook until browned on all sides; work in batches, if necessary.

Return the onion mixture to the casserole with all the lamb. Stir in the stock, wine, vinegar, tomatoes with their juices, and salt and pepper to taste. Bring to a boil, scraping any glazed bits from the bottom of the casserole. Reduce the heat and stir in the thyme, bay leaves, and paprika.

Transfer to a preheated oven, 325°F/160°C, and cook, covered, for 40–45 minutes until the lamb is tender. Stir in the chickpeas and return to the oven, uncovered, for 10 minutes, or until they are heated through and the juices are reduced.

Taste and adjust the seasoning. Garnish with thyme and serve.

SERVES 4–6

6 tbsp olive oil

8 oz/225 g chorizo sausage, cut into ¼-inch/5-mm thick slices, casings removed

2 large onions, chopped

6 large garlic cloves, crushed

2 lb/900 g boned leg of lamb, cut into 2-inch/5-cm chunks

scant 1¼ cups lamb stock or water

½ cup red wine, such as Rioja or Tempranillo

2 tbsp sherry vinegar

1 lb 12 oz/800 g canned chopped tomatoes

4 sprigs fresh thyme, plus extra to garnish

2 bay leaves

½ tsp sweet Spanish paprika

1 lb 12 oz/800 g canned chickpeas, rinsed and drained

salt and pepper

IRISH STEW

Preheat the oven to 325°F/160°C. Spread the flour on a plate and season with salt and pepper. Roll the pieces of lamb in the flour to coat, shaking off any excess, and arrange in the bottom of a casserole.

Layer the onions, carrots, and potatoes on top of the lamb.

Sprinkle in the thyme and pour in the stock, then cover and cook in the preheated oven for 2½ hours. Garnish with the chopped parsley and serve straight from the casserole.

SERVES 4

4 tbsp all-purpose flour

3 lb/1.3 kg middle neck of lamb, trimmed of visible fat, cut into chunks

3 large onions, chopped

3 carrots, sliced

1 lb/450 g potatoes, cut into quarters

½ tsp dried thyme

scant 3½ cups hot beef stock

salt and pepper

2 tbsp chopped fresh parsley, to garnish

LAMB SHANKS

Dry-roast the coriander and cumin seeds until fragrant, then pound with the cinnamon, chile, and 2 garlic cloves in a mortar and pestle. Stir in half the oil and the lime rind. Rub the spice paste all over the lamb and marinate for 4 hours.

Preheat the oven to 400°F/200°C. Heat the remaining oil in a flameproof casserole and cook the lamb, turning frequently, until evenly browned. Chop the remaining garlic and add to the casserole with the onions, carrots, celery, and lime, then pour in enough stock or water to cover. Stir in the tomato paste, add the herbs, and season with salt and pepper.

Cover and cook in the preheated oven for 30 minutes. Reduce the oven temperature to 325°F/160°C and cook for an additional 3 hours, or until very tender.

Transfer the lamb to a dish. Strain the cooking liquid to remove any solids, then return the liquid to the casserole. Boil until reduced and thickened. Serve the lamb with the sauce poured over it, garnished with sprigs of rosemary.

SERVES 6

1 tsp coriander seeds

1 tsp cumin seeds

1 tsp ground cinnamon

1 fresh green chile, seeded and finely chopped

1 garlic bulb, separated into cloves

½ cup peanut oil or sunflower oil

grated rind of 1 lime

6 lamb shanks

2 onions, chopped

2 carrots, chopped

2 celery stalks, chopped

1 lime, chopped

3 cups beef stock or water

1 tsp sun-dried tomato paste

2 fresh mint sprigs

2 fresh rosemary sprigs, plus extra to garnish

salt and pepper

POULTRY

ITALIAN-STYLE ROAST CHICKEN

Rinse the chicken inside and out with cold water and drain well. Carefully cut between the skin and the top of the breast meat using a small pointed knife. Slide a finger into the slit and carefully enlarge it to form a pocket. Continue until the skin is completely lifted away from both breasts and the top of the legs.

Chop the leaves from 3 rosemary stems. Mix with the feta cheese, sun-dried tomato paste, butter, and pepper to taste, then spoon under the skin. Put the chicken in a large roasting pan, cover with foil, and cook in a preheated oven, 375°F/190°C, for 20 minutes per 1 lb 2 oz/500 g, plus 20 minutes.

Break the garlic bulb into cloves but do not peel. Add the vegetables and garlic to the chicken after 40 minutes, drizzle with oil, tuck in a few stems of rosemary, and season with salt and pepper. Cook for the remaining calculated time, removing the foil for the last 40 minutes to brown the chicken.

Transfer the chicken to a serving platter. Place some of the vegetables around the chicken and transfer the remainder to a warmed serving dish. Spoon the fat (it will be floating on top) out of the roasting pan and stir the flour into the remaining cooking juices. Place the roasting pan on top of the stove and cook over medium heat for 2 minutes, then gradually stir in the stock. Bring to a boil, stirring, until thickened. Strain into a sauce boat and serve with the chicken.

SERVES 6

5 lb 8 oz/2.5 kg chicken

sprigs of fresh rosemary

3/4 cup coarsely grated feta cheese

2 tbsp sun-dried tomato paste

4 tbsp butter, softened

1 bulb garlic

2 lb 4 oz/1 kg new potatoes, halved if large

1 each red, green, and yellow bell pepper, seeded and cut into chunks

3 zucchini, thinly sliced

2 tbsp olive oil

2 tbsp all-purpose flour

2 1/2 cups chicken stock

salt and pepper

CHICKEN IN WHITE WINE

Preheat the oven to 325°F/160°C. Melt half the butter with the oil in a flameproof casserole. Add the bacon and cook over medium heat, stirring, for 5–10 minutes, or until golden brown. Transfer the bacon to a large plate. Add the onions and garlic to the casserole and cook over low heat, stirring occasionally, for 10 minutes, or until golden. Transfer to the plate. Add the chicken and cook over medium heat, stirring constantly, for 8–10 minutes, or until golden. Transfer to the plate.

Drain off any excess fat from the casserole. Stir in the wine and stock and bring to a boil, scraping any sediment off the bottom. Add the bouquet garni and season to taste. Return the bacon, onions, and chicken to the casserole. Cover and cook in the preheated oven for 1 hour. Add the mushrooms, re-cover, and cook for 15 minutes. Meanwhile, make a beurre manié by mashing the remaining butter with the flour in a small bowl.

Remove the casserole from the oven and set over medium heat. Remove and discard the bouquet garni. Whisk in the beurre manié, a little at a time. Bring to a boil, stirring constantly, then serve, garnished with fresh herb sprigs.

SERVES 4

¼ cup butter

2 tbsp olive oil

2 thick, rindless, lean bacon strips, chopped

4 oz/115 g pearl onions, peeled

1 garlic clove, finely chopped

4 lb/1.8 kg chicken pieces

1¾ cups dry white wine

1¼ cups chicken stock

1 bouquet garni

4 oz/115 g button mushrooms

2½ tbsp all-purpose flour

salt and pepper

fresh mixed herbs, to garnish

COQ AU VIN

Melt half the butter with the olive oil in a large, flameproof casserole. Add the chicken and cook over medium heat, stirring, for 8–10 minutes, or until golden brown. Add the bacon, onions, mushrooms, and garlic.

Pour in the brandy and set it alight with a match or taper. When the flames have died down, add the wine, stock, and bouquet garni, and season to taste with salt and pepper. Bring to a boil, reduce the heat, and simmer gently for 1 hour, or until the chicken pieces are cooked through and tender. Meanwhile, make a beurre manié by mashing the remaining butter with the flour in a small bowl.

Remove and discard the bouquet garni. Transfer the chicken to a large plate and keep warm. Stir the beurre manié into the casserole, a little at a time. Bring to a boil, return the chicken to the casserole, and serve immediately, garnished with bay leaves.

SERVES 4

¼ cup butter

2 tbsp olive oil

4 lb/1.8 kg chicken pieces

4 oz/115 g rindless smoked bacon, cut into strips

4 oz/115 g pearl onions, peeled

4 oz/115 g cremini mushrooms, halved

2 garlic cloves, finely chopped

2 tbsp brandy

scant 1 cup red wine

1¼ cups chicken stock

1 bouquet garni

2 tbsp all-purpose flour

salt and pepper

bay leaves, to garnish

HUNTER'S CHICKEN

Preheat the oven to 325°F/160°C. Heat the butter and oil in a flameproof casserole and cook the chicken over medium–high heat, turning frequently, for 10 minutes, or until golden all over and seared. Using a slotted spoon, transfer to a plate.

Add the onions and garlic to the casserole and cook over low heat, stirring occasionally, for 10 minutes, or until softened and golden. Add the tomatoes with their juice, the herbs, sun-dried tomato paste, and wine, and season to taste with salt and pepper. Bring to a boil, then return the chicken portions to the casserole, pushing them down into the sauce.

Cover and cook in the preheated oven for 50 minutes. Add the mushrooms and cook for an additional 10 minutes, or until the chicken is tender and the juices run clear when a skewer is inserted into the thickest part of the meat. Serve immediately.

SERVES 4

1 tbsp unsalted butter

2 tbsp olive oil

4 lb/1.8 kg skinned chicken portions

2 red onions, sliced

2 garlic cloves, finely chopped

14 oz/400 g canned chopped tomatoes

2 tbsp chopped fresh flat-leaf parsley

6 fresh basil leaves, torn

1 tbsp sun-dried tomato paste

²/₃ cup red wine

8 oz/225 g button mushrooms, sliced

salt and pepper

CHICKEN RISOTTO WITH SAFFRON

Melt 2 oz/55 g of the butter in a deep pan, add the chicken and onion, and cook, stirring frequently, for 8 minutes, or until golden brown.

Add the rice and mix to coat in the butter. Cook, stirring constantly, for 2–3 minutes, or until the grains are translucent. Add the wine and cook, stirring constantly, for 1 minute until reduced.

Mix the saffron with 4 tablespoons of the hot stock. Add the liquid to the rice and cook, stirring constantly, until it is absorbed.

Gradually add the remaining hot stock, a ladleful at a time. Stir constantly and add more liquid as the rice absorbs each addition. Cook for 20 minutes, or until all the liquid is absorbed and the rice is creamy. Season to taste.

Remove the risotto from the heat and add the remaining butter. Mix well, then stir in the Parmesan until it melts. Spoon the risotto onto warmed plates and serve at once.

SERVES 4

4½ oz/125 g butter

2 lb/900 g skinless, boneless chicken breasts, thinly sliced

1 large onion, chopped

1 lb 2 oz/500 g risotto rice

⅔ cup white wine

1 tsp crumbled saffron threads

generous 5½ cups boiling chicken stock

½ cup freshly grated Parmesan cheese

salt and pepper

PAPPARDELLE WITH CHICKEN & PORCINI

Place the porcini in a small bowl, add the hot water, and let soak for 20 minutes. Meanwhile, place the tomatoes and their can juices in a heavy-bottom pan and break them up with a wooden spoon, then stir in the chile. Bring to a boil, reduce the heat, and simmer, stirring occasionally, for 30 minutes, or until reduced.

Remove the mushrooms from their soaking liquid with a slotted spoon, reserving the liquid. Strain the liquid through a coffee filter paper or cheesecloth-lined strainer into the tomatoes and simmer for an additional 15 minutes.

Meanwhile, heat 2 tablespoons of the olive oil in a heavy-bottom skillet. Add the chicken and cook, stirring frequently, until golden brown all over and tender. Stir in the mushrooms and garlic and cook for 5 minutes.

While the chicken is cooking, bring a large, heavy-bottom pan of lightly salted water to a boil. Add the pasta, return to a boil, and cook for 8–10 minutes, or until tender but still firm to the bite. Drain well, transfer to a warmed serving dish, drizzle with the remaining olive oil, and toss lightly. Stir the chicken mixture into the tomato sauce, season to taste with salt and pepper, and spoon onto the pasta. Toss lightly, sprinkle with parsley, and serve immediately.

SERVES 4

3/8 cup dried porcini mushrooms

3/4 cup hot water

1 lb 12 oz/800 g canned chopped tomatoes

1 fresh red chile, seeded and finely chopped

3 tbsp olive oil

12 oz/350 g skinless, boneless chicken, cut into thin strips

2 garlic cloves, finely chopped

12 oz/350 g dried pappardelle

salt and pepper

2 tbsp chopped fresh flat-leaf parsley, to garnish

LOUISIANA CHICKEN

Heat the oil in a large, heavy-bottom saucepan or flameproof casserole. Add the chicken and cook over medium heat, stirring, for 5–10 minutes or until golden. Transfer the chicken to a plate with a slotted spoon.

Stir the flour into the oil and cook over very low heat, stirring constantly, for 15 minutes, or until light golden. Do not let it burn. Immediately add the onion, celery, and green bell pepper and cook, stirring constantly, for 2 minutes. Add the garlic, thyme, and chiles and cook, stirring, for 1 minute.

Stir in the tomatoes and their juices, then gradually stir in the stock. Return the chicken pieces to the pan, cover, and simmer for 45 minutes, or until the chicken is cooked through and tender. Season to taste with salt and pepper, transfer to warmed serving plates, and serve immediately, garnished with some lamb's lettuce and a sprinkling of chopped thyme.

SERVES 4

5 tbsp corn oil

4 chicken pieces

6 tbsp all-purpose flour

1 onion, chopped

2 celery stalks, sliced

1 green bell pepper, seeded and chopped

2 garlic cloves, finely chopped

2 tsp chopped fresh thyme

2 fresh red chiles, seeded and finely chopped

14 oz/400 g canned chopped tomatoes

1¼ cups chicken stock

salt and pepper

lamb's lettuce and chopped fresh thyme, to garnish

CHICKEN TAGINE

Heat the oil in a large pan over medium heat, add the onion and garlic and cook for 3 minutes, stirring frequently. Add the chicken and cook, stirring constantly, for an additional 5 minutes, or until seared on all sides. Add the cumin and cinnamon sticks to the pan halfway through searing the chicken.

Sprinkle in the flour and cook, stirring constantly, for 2 minutes. Add the eggplant, red bell pepper, and mushrooms and cook for an additional 2 minutes, stirring constantly.

Blend the tomato paste with the stock, stir into the pan, and bring to a boil. Reduce the heat and add the chickpeas and apricots. Cover and let simmer for 15–20 minutes, or until the chicken is tender.

Season with salt and pepper to taste and serve at once, sprinkled with cilantro.

SERVES 4

1 tbsp olive oil

1 onion, cut into small wedges

2–4 garlic cloves, sliced

1 lb/450 g skinless, boneless chicken breast, diced

1 tsp ground cumin

2 cinnamon sticks, lightly bruised

1 tbsp whole wheat flour

8 oz/225 g eggplant, diced

1 red bell pepper, seeded and chopped

3 oz/85 g button mushrooms, sliced

1 tbsp tomato paste

2½ cups chicken stock

10 oz/280 g canned chickpeas, drained and rinsed

⅓ cup no-soak dried apricots, chopped

salt and pepper

1 tbsp chopped fresh cilantro, to garnish

BALTI CHICKEN

Heat the ghee in a large, heavy-bottom skillet. Add the onions and cook over low heat, stirring occasionally, for 10 minutes, or until golden. Add the sliced tomatoes, nigella seeds, peppercorns, cardamom, cinnamon stick, chili powder, garam masala, garlic paste, and ginger paste, and season with salt to taste. Cook, stirring constantly, for 5 minutes.

Add the chicken and cook, stirring constantly, for 5 minutes, or until well coated in the spice paste. Stir in the yogurt. Cover and let simmer, stirring occasionally, for 10 minutes.

Stir in the chopped cilantro, chiles, and lime juice. Transfer to a warmed serving dish, sprinkle with more chopped cilantro, and serve immediately.

SERVES 6

3 tbsp ghee or vegetable oil

2 large onions, sliced

3 tomatoes, sliced

½ tsp nigella seeds

4 black peppercorns

2 cardamom pods

1 cinnamon stick

1 tsp chili powder

1 tsp garam masala

1 tsp garlic paste

1 tsp ginger paste

1 lb 9 oz/700 g skinless, boneless chicken breasts or thighs, diced

2 tbsp plain yogurt

2 tbsp chopped fresh cilantro, plus extra to garnish

2 fresh green chiles, seeded and finely chopped

2 tbsp lime juice

salt

THAI GREEN CHICKEN CURRY

Heat the oil in a preheated wok or large, heavy-bottom skillet. Add 2 tablespoons of the curry paste and stir-fry briefly until all the aromas are released.

Add the chicken, lime leaves, and lemongrass and stir-fry for 3–4 minutes, until the meat is starting to color. Add the coconut milk and eggplants and let simmer gently for 8–10 minutes, or until tender.

Stir in the fish sauce and serve at once, garnished with Thai basil sprigs and lime leaves.

SERVES 4

2 tbsp peanut oil or corn oil

2 tbsp Thai green curry paste

1 lb 2 oz/500 g skinless boneless chicken breasts, cut into cubes

2 kaffir lime leaves, coarsely torn

1 lemongrass stalk, finely chopped

1 cup canned coconut milk

16 baby eggplants, halved

2 tbsp Thai fish sauce

fresh Thai basil sprigs and thinly sliced kaffir lime leaves, to garnish

ITALIAN TURKEY CUTLETS

Heat the oil in a flameproof casserole or heavy-bottom skillet. Add the turkey scallops and cook over medium heat for 5–10 minutes, turning occasionally, until golden. Transfer to a plate.

Seed and slice the red bell peppers. Slice the onion, add to the skillet with the bell peppers, and cook over low heat, stirring occasionally, for 5 minutes, or until softened. Add the garlic and cook for an additional 2 minutes.

Return the turkey to the skillet and add the strained tomatoes, wine, and marjoram. Season to taste. Bring to a boil, then reduce the heat, cover, and simmer, stirring occasionally, for 25–30 minutes, or until the turkey is cooked through and tender.

Stir in the cannellini beans. Simmer for an additional 5 minutes. Sprinkle the breadcrumbs over the top and place under a preheated medium-hot broiler for 2–3 minutes, or until golden. Serve, garnished with basil.

SERVES 4

1 tbsp olive oil

4 turkey scallops or steaks

2 red bell peppers

1 red onion

2 garlic cloves, finely chopped

1¼ cups strained tomatoes

⅔ cup medium white wine

1 tbsp chopped fresh marjoram

14 oz/400 g canned cannellini beans, drained and rinsed

3 tbsp fresh white breadcrumbs

salt and pepper

fresh basil sprigs, to garnish

MEXICAN TURKEY

Preheat the oven to 325°F/160°C. Spread the flour on a plate and season with salt and pepper. Coat the turkey fillets in the seasoned flour, shaking off any excess.

Heat the oil in a flameproof casserole. Add the turkey fillets and cook over medium heat, turning occasionally, for 5–10 minutes, or until golden. Transfer to a plate with a slotted spoon.

Add the onion and bell pepper to the casserole. Cook over low heat, stirring occasionally, for 5 minutes, or until softened. Sprinkle in any remaining seasoned flour and cook, stirring constantly, for 1 minute. Gradually stir in the stock, then add the raisins, chopped tomatoes, chili powder, cinnamon, cumin, and chocolate. Season to taste with salt and pepper. Bring to a boil, stirring constantly.

Return the turkey to the casserole, cover, and cook in the preheated oven for 50 minutes. Serve immediately, garnished with sprigs of cilantro.

SERVES 4

6 tbsp all-purpose flour

4 turkey breast fillets

3 tbsp corn oil

1 onion, thinly sliced

1 red bell pepper, seeded and sliced

1¼ cups chicken stock

2 tbsp raisins

4 tomatoes, peeled, seeded, and chopped

1 tsp chili powder

½ tsp ground cinnamon

pinch of ground cumin

1 oz/25 g semisweet chocolate, finely chopped or grated

salt and pepper

sprigs of fresh cilantro, to garnish

DUCK LEGS
WITH OLIVES

Put the duck legs in the bottom of a flameproof casserole or a large, heavy-bottom skillet with a tight-fitting lid. Add the tomatoes, garlic, onion, carrot, celery, thyme, and olives, and stir together. Season with salt and pepper to taste.

Turn the heat to high and cook, uncovered, until the ingredients start to bubble. Reduce the heat to low, cover tightly, and let simmer for 1¼–1½ hours, until the duck is very tender. Check occasionally and add a little water if the mixture appears to be drying out.

When the duck is tender, transfer it to a serving platter, cover, and keep hot in a preheated warm oven. Leave the casserole uncovered, increase the heat to medium, and cook, stirring, for about 10 minutes until the mixture forms a sauce. Stir in the orange rind, then taste and adjust the seasoning if necessary.

Mash the tender garlic cloves with a fork and spread over the duck legs. Spoon the sauce over the top. Serve at once.

SERVES 4

4 duck legs, all visible fat trimmed off

1 lb 12 oz/800 g canned tomatoes, chopped

8 garlic cloves, peeled but left whole

1 large onion, chopped

1 carrot, peeled and finely chopped

1 celery stalk, peeled and finely chopped

3 sprigs fresh thyme

generous ½ cup Spanish green olives in brine, stuffed with pimientos, garlic, or almonds, drained and rinsed

1 tsp finely grated orange rind

salt and pepper

DUCK JAMBALAYA-STYLE STEW

Remove and discard the skin and any fat from the duck breasts. Cut the flesh into bite-size pieces.

Heat half the oil in a large, deep skillet and cook the duck, ham, and chorizo over high heat, stirring frequently, for 5 minutes, or until browned on all sides and seared. Using a slotted spoon, remove from the skillet and set aside.

Add the onion, garlic, celery, and chiles to the skillet and cook over medium heat, stirring frequently, for 5 minutes, or until softened. Add the green bell pepper, then stir in the stock, oregano, tomatoes, and hot pepper sauce.

Bring to a boil, then reduce the heat and return the duck, ham, and chorizo to the skillet. Cover and simmer, stirring occasionally, for 20 minutes, or until the duck and ham are tender.

Serve immediately, garnished with parsley and accompanied by salad greens and rice.

SERVES 4

4 duck breasts, about 5½ oz/150 g each

2 tbsp olive oil

8 oz/225 g piece ham, cut into small chunks

8 oz/225 g chorizo, outer casing removed, cut into chunks

1 onion, chopped

3 garlic cloves, chopped

3 celery stalks, chopped

1–2 fresh red chiles, seeded and chopped

1 green bell pepper, seeded and chopped

2½ cups chicken stock

1 tbsp chopped fresh oregano

14 oz/400 g canned chopped tomatoes

1–2 tsp hot pepper sauce, or to taste

chopped fresh parsley, to garnish

salad greens and freshly cooked long-grain rice, to serve

FISH & SEAFOOD

MONKFISH PARCELS

Preheat the oven to 375°F/190°C. Cut 4 large pieces of foil, about 9-inches/23-cm square. Brush lightly with a little of the oil, then divide the zucchini and bell pepper among them.

Rinse the fish fillets under cold running water and pat dry with paper towels. Cut them in half, then put 1 piece on top of each pile of zucchini and bell pepper. Cut the bacon slices in half and lay 3 pieces across each piece of fish. Season to taste with salt and pepper, drizzle over the remaining oil, and close up the packages. Seal tightly, transfer to an ovenproof dish, and bake in the preheated oven for 25 minutes.

Remove from the oven, open each foil package slightly, and serve with pasta and slices of olive bread.

SERVES 4

4 tsp olive oil

2 zucchini, sliced

1 large red bell pepper, peeled, seeded, and cut into strips

2 monkfish fillets, about 4½ oz/125 g each, skin and membrane removed

6 smoked lean bacon slices

salt and pepper

freshly cooked pasta and slices of olive bread, to serve

ROASTED MONKFISH

Preheat the oven to 400°F/200°C. Remove the central bone from the fish if not already removed and make small slits down each fillet. Cut 2 of the garlic cloves into thin slivers and insert into the fish. Place the fish on a sheet of wax paper, season with salt and pepper to taste, and drizzle over 1 tablespoon of the oil. Bring the top edges together. Form into a pleat and fold over, then fold the ends underneath, completely encasing the fish. Set aside.

Put the remaining garlic cloves and all the vegetables into a roasting pan and drizzle with the remaining oil, turning the vegetables so that they are well coated in the oil.

Roast in the preheated oven for 20 minutes, turning occasionally. Put the fish package on top of the vegetables and cook for an additional 15–20 minutes, or until the vegetables are tender and the fish is cooked.

Remove from the oven and open up the package. Cut the monkfish into thick slices. Arrange the vegetables on warmed serving plates, top with the fish slices, and sprinkle with the basil. Serve at once.

SERVES 4

1 lb 8 oz/675 g monkfish tail, skinned

4–5 large garlic cloves, peeled

3 tbsp olive oil

1 onion, cut into wedges

1 small eggplant, about 10½ oz/300 g, cut into chunks

1 red bell pepper, seeded, cut into wedges

1 yellow bell pepper, seeded, cut into wedges

1 large zucchini, about 8 oz/225 g, cut into wedges

salt and pepper

1 tbsp shredded fresh basil, to garnish

MEDITERRANEAN SWORDFISH

Heat the oil in a large, heavy-bottom skillet. Add the onion and celery and cook over low heat, stirring occasionally, for 5 minutes, or until softened.

Meanwhile, coarsely chop half the olives. Stir the chopped and whole olives into the pan with the tomatoes and capers and season to taste with salt and pepper.

Bring to a boil, then reduce the heat, cover, and simmer gently, stirring occasionally, for 15 minutes.

Add the swordfish steaks to the pan and return to a boil. Cover and simmer, turning the fish once, for 20 minutes, or until the fish is cooked and the flesh flakes easily. Transfer the fish to serving plates and spoon the sauce over them. Garnish with parsley and serve immediately.

SERVES 4

2 tbsp olive oil

1 onion, finely chopped

1 celery stalk, finely chopped

4 oz/115 g green olives, pitted

1 lb/450 g tomatoes, chopped

3 tbsp bottled capers, drained

4 swordfish steaks,
    about 5 oz/140 g each

salt and pepper

fresh flat-leaf parsley sprigs,
    to garnish

SICILIAN TUNA

Whisk all the marinade ingredients together in a small bowl. Put the tuna steaks in a large, shallow dish and spoon over 4 tablespoons of the marinade, turning until well coated. Cover and let marinate in the refrigerator for 30 minutes. Set aside the remaining marinade.

Heat a stovetop ridged grill pan over high heat. Put the fennel and onions in a separate bowl, add the oil, and toss well to coat. Add to the grill pan and cook for 5 minutes on each side until just beginning to color. Transfer to 4 warmed serving plates, drizzle with the reserved marinade, and keep warm.

Add the tuna steaks to the grill pan and cook, turning once, for 4–5 minutes until firm to the touch but still moist inside. Transfer the tuna to the serving plates and serve at once with crusty rolls.

SERVES 4

4 tuna steaks, about
  5 oz/140 g each

2 fennel bulbs, thickly sliced
  lengthwise

2 red onions, sliced

2 tbsp extra virgin olive oil

crusty rolls, to serve

marinade

½ cup extra virgin olive oil

4 garlic cloves, finely chopped

4 fresh red chiles, seeded and
  finely chopped

juice and finely grated rind of
  2 lemons

4 tbsp finely chopped fresh
  flat-leaf parsley

salt and pepper

CATALAN FISH STEW

Put the saffron threads in a heatproof pitcher with the water and set aside for at least 10 minutes to infuse.

Heat the oil in a large, heavy-bottom flameproof casserole over medium-high heat. Reduce the heat to low and cook the onion, stirring occasionally, for 10 minutes, or until golden but not browned. Stir in the garlic, thyme, bay leaves, and red bell peppers and cook, stirring frequently, for 5 minutes, or until the bell peppers are softened and the onions have softened further.

Add the tomatoes and paprika and simmer, stirring frequently, for an additional 5 minutes.

Stir in the stock, the saffron and its soaking liquid, and the almonds and bring to a boil, stirring. Reduce the heat and simmer for 5–10 minutes, or until the sauce reduces and thickens. Season to taste with salt and pepper.

Meanwhile, clean the mussels and clams by scrubbing or scraping the shells and pulling out any beards that are attached to the mussels. Discard any with broken shells or any that refuse to close when tapped.

Gently stir the hake into the stew so that it doesn't break up, then add the shrimp, mussels, and clams. Reduce the heat to very low, then cover and simmer for 5 minutes, or until the hake is opaque, the mussels and clams have opened, and the shrimp have turned pink. Discard any mussels or clams that remain closed. Remove the bay leaf and serve immediately.

SERVES 4–6

large pinch of saffron threads

4 tbsp almost boiling water

6 tbsp olive oil

1 large onion, chopped

2 garlic cloves, finely chopped

1½ tbsp chopped fresh thyme leaves

2 bay leaves

2 red bell peppers, seeded and coarsely chopped

1 lb 12 oz/800 g canned chopped tomatoes

1 tsp smoked paprika

1 cup fish stock

1 cup blanched almonds, toasted and finely ground

12–16 live mussels

12–16 live clams

1 lb 5 oz/600 g thick boned hake or cod fillets, skinned and cut into 2-inch/5-cm chunks

12–16 raw shrimp, shelled and deveined

salt and pepper

SHRIMP LAKSA

Shell and devein the shrimp. Put the fish stock, salt, and the shrimp heads, shells, and tails in a large saucepan over high heat and slowly bring to a boil. Lower the heat and simmer for 10 minutes, then remove from the heat. Transfer to a bowl and keep warm

Meanwhile, make the laksa paste. Put all the ingredients except the oil in a food processor and blend. With the motor running, slowly add up to 2 tablespoons of oil just until a paste forms. (If your food processor is too large to work efficiently with this small quantity, use a mortar and pestle, or make double the quantity and keep leftovers tightly covered in the refrigerator to use another time.)

Heat the oil in the cleaned large saucepan over high heat. Add the paste and stir-fry until it is fragrant. Strain the stock through a strainer lined with cheesecloth. Stir the stock into the laksa paste, along with the coconut milk, nam pla, and lime juice. Bring to a boil, then lower the heat, cover, and simmer for 30 minutes.

Meanwhile, soak the noodles in a large bowl with enough lukewarm water to cover for 20 minutes, until soft. Alternatively, cook according to the package instructions. Drain and set aside.

Add the shrimp and bean sprouts to the soup and continue simmering just until the shrimp turn opaque and curl. Divide the noodles among 4 bowls and ladle the soup over, making sure everyone gets an equal share of the shrimp. Garnish with the cilantro and serve.

SERVES 4

20–24 large raw unshelled shrimp

2 cups fish stock

pinch of salt

1 tsp peanut oil

2 cups coconut milk

2 tsp nam pla (Thai fish sauce)

½ tbsp lime juice

4 oz/115 g dried medium rice
  noodles

⅜ cup bean sprouts

sprigs of fresh cilantro, to garnish

laksa paste

6 fresh cilantro stalks with leaves

3 large garlic cloves, crushed

1 fresh red chile, seeded and
  chopped

1 lemongrass stalk, center part
  only, chopped

1-inch/2.5-cm piece fresh ginger,
  peeled and chopped

1½ tbsp shrimp paste

½ tsp ground turmeric

2 tbsp peanut oil

SHRIMP WITH COCONUT RICE

Place the mushrooms in a small bowl, cover with hot water, and set aside to soak for 30 minutes. Drain, then cut off and discard the stalks and slice the caps.

Heat the oil in a wok and stir-fry the scallions, coconut, and chile for 2–3 minutes, until lightly browned. Add the mushrooms and stir-fry for 3–4 minutes.

Add the rice and stir-fry for 2–3 minutes, then add the stock and bring to a boil. Reduce the heat and add the coconut milk. Let simmer for 10–15 minutes, until the rice is tender. Stir in the shrimp and basil, heat through, and serve.

SERVES 4

1 cup dried Chinese mushrooms

1 tbsp vegetable oil or peanut oil

6 scallions, chopped

scant ½ cup dry unsweetened coconut

1 fresh green chile, seeded and chopped

generous 1 cup jasmine rice

⅔ cup fish stock

1¾ cups coconut milk

12 oz/350 g cooked shelled shrimp

6 sprigs fresh Thai basil

SHRIMP & CHICKEN PAELLA

Soak the mussels in lightly salted water for 10 minutes. Put the saffron threads and water in a small bowl or cup and let infuse for a few minutes. Meanwhile, put the rice in a strainer and rinse in cold water until the water runs clear. Set aside.

Heat 3 tablespoons of the oil in a 12-inch/30-cm paella pan or ovenproof casserole. Add the chicken thighs and cook over medium–high heat, turning frequently, for 5 minutes, or until golden and crispy. Using a slotted spoon, transfer to a bowl. Add the chorizo to the pan and cook, stirring, for 1 minute, or until beginning to crisp. Add to the chicken.

Heat the remaining oil in the pan and cook the onions, stirring frequently, for 2 minutes, then add the garlic and paprika and cook for an additional 3 minutes, or until the onions are soft but not browned.

Add the drained rice, beans, and peas and stir until coated in oil. Return the chicken and chorizo and any accumulated juices to the pan. Stir in the stock, saffron and its soaking liquid, and salt and pepper to taste and bring to a boil, stirring constantly. Reduce the heat to low and let simmer, uncovered and without stirring, for 15 minutes, or until the rice is almost tender and most of the liquid has been absorbed.

Arrange the mussels, shrimp, and red bell peppers on top, then cover and simmer, without stirring, for an additional 5 minutes, or until the shrimp turn pink and the mussels open. Discard any mussels that remain closed. Taste and adjust the seasoning if necessary. Sprinkle with the parsley and serve immediately.

SERVES 6–8

16 live mussels

½ tsp saffron threads

2 tbsp hot water

generous 1¾ cups paella rice

6 tbsp olive oil

6–8 unboned, skin-on chicken thighs

5 oz/140 g Spanish chorizo sausage, sliced

2 large onions, chopped

4 large garlic cloves, crushed

1 tsp mild or hot Spanish paprika

3½ oz/100 g green beans, chopped

generous ¾ cup frozen peas

5 cups fish stock

16 raw shrimp, shelled and deveined

2 red bell peppers, halved and seeded, then broiled, peeled, and sliced

salt and pepper

1¼ oz/35 g fresh parsley, chopped, to garnish

MOULES MARINIÈRES

Clean the mussels by scrubbing or scraping the shells and pulling off any beards. Discard any with broken shells or any that refuse to close when tapped with a knife. Rinse the mussels under cold running water.

Pour the wine into a large, heavy-bottom pan, add the shallots and bouquet garni, and season to taste with pepper. Bring to a boil over medium heat. Add the mussels, cover tightly, and cook, shaking the pan occasionally, for 5 minutes. Remove and discard the bouquet garni and any mussels that remain closed. Divide the mussels among 4 soup plates with a slotted spoon. Tilt the casserole to let any sediment settle, then spoon the cooking liquid over the mussels. Garnish with the bay leaves and serve immediately with bread.

SERVES 4

4 lb 8 oz/2 kg live mussels

1¼ cups dry white wine

6 shallots, finely chopped

1 bouquet garni

pepper

4 bay leaves, to garnish

crusty bread, to serve

SQUID WITH PARSLEY & PINE NUTS

Place the golden raisins in a small bowl, cover with lukewarm water, and set aside for 15 minutes to plump up.

Meanwhile, heat the olive oil in a heavy-bottom pan. Add the parsley and garlic and cook over low heat, stirring frequently, for 3 minutes. Add the squid and cook, stirring occasionally, for 5 minutes.

Increase the heat to medium, pour in the wine, and cook until it has almost completely evaporated. Stir in the strained tomatoes and season to taste with chili powder and salt. Reduce the heat again, cover, and let simmer gently, stirring occasionally, for 45–50 minutes, until the squid is almost tender.

Drain the golden raisins and stir them into the pan with the pine nuts. Let simmer for an additional 10 minutes, then serve immediately garnished with the reserved chopped parsley.

SERVES 4

½ cup golden raisins

5 tbsp olive oil

2 tbsp chopped fresh flat-leaf parsley, plus extra to garnish

2 garlic cloves, finely chopped

1 lb 12 oz/800 g prepared squid, sliced, or squid rings

½ cup dry white wine

1 lb 2 oz/500 g strained tomatoes

pinch of chili powder

¾ cup finely chopped pine nuts

salt

SEARED SCALLOPS IN GARLIC BROTH

Combine the garlic cloves, celery, carrot, onion, peppercorns, parsley stems, and water in a saucepan with a good pinch of salt. Bring to a boil, reduce the heat, and simmer, partially covered, for 30–45 minutes.

Strain the stock into a bowl, clean the saucepan, then return the stock to the pan. Taste and adjust the seasoning, and keep hot.

If using sea scallops, slice in half to form 2 thinner rounds from each. (If the scallops are very large, slice them into 3 rounds.) Sprinkle with salt and pepper.

Heat the oil in a skillet over medium–high heat and cook the scallops on one side for 1–2 minutes, until lightly browned and the flesh becomes opaque.

Divide the scallops among 4 warmed shallow bowls, arranging them browned-side up. Ladle the soup over the scallops, then float a few cilantro leaves on top. Serve immediately.

SERVES 4

1 large garlic bulb (about 3½ oz/ 100 g), separated into unpeeled cloves

1 celery stalk, chopped

1 carrot, chopped

1 onion, chopped

10 peppercorns

5–6 parsley stems

5 cups water

8 oz/225 g large sea scallops

1 tbsp oil

salt and pepper

fresh cilantro leaves, to garnish

ROASTED
SEAFOOD

Preheat the oven to 400°F/200°C. Place the potatoes in a large roasting pan together with the onions, zucchini, garlic, lemons, and rosemary sprigs.

Pour over the oil and toss to coat all the vegetables in it. Roast in the oven for 30 minutes, turning occasionally, until the potatoes are tender.

Once the potatoes are tender, add the shrimp, squid, and tomatoes, tossing to coat them in the oil, and roast for 10 minutes. All the vegetables should be cooked through and slightly charred for full flavor. Transfer the roasted seafood and vegetables to warmed serving plates and serve hot.

SERVES 4

1 lb 5 oz/600 g new potatoes, scrubbed and parboiled for 10–15 minutes

3 red onions, cut into wedges

2 zucchini, cut into chunks

8 garlic cloves, peeled but left whole

2 lemons, cut into wedges

4 fresh rosemary sprigs

4 tbsp olive oil

12 oz/350 g unshelled raw shrimp

2 small raw squid, cut into rings

4 tomatoes, quartered

MOROCCAN
FISH TAGINE

Heat the olive oil in a flameproof casserole. Add the onion and cook gently over very low heat, stirring occasionally, for 10 minutes, or until softened, but not colored. Add the saffron, cinnamon, ground coriander, cumin, and turmeric and cook for an additional 30 seconds, stirring constantly.

Add the tomatoes and fish stock and stir well. Bring to a boil, reduce the heat, cover, and simmer for 15 minutes. Uncover and simmer for 20–35 minutes, or until thickened.

Cut each red snapper in half, then add the fish pieces to the casserole, pushing them down into the liquid. Simmer the stew for an additional 5–6 minutes, or until the fish is just cooked.

Carefully stir in the olives, lemon, and fresh cilantro. Season to taste with salt and pepper and serve immediately with couscous.

SERVES 4

2 tbsp olive oil

1 large onion, finely chopped

pinch of saffron threads

½ tsp ground cinnamon

1 tsp ground coriander

½ tsp ground cumin

½ tsp ground turmeric

7 oz/200 g canned chopped
    tomatoes

1¼ cups fish stock

4 small red snappers, cleaned,
    boned, and heads and tails
    removed

2 oz/55 g pitted green olives

1 tbsp chopped preserved lemon

3 tbsp chopped fresh cilantro

salt and pepper

freshly cooked couscous,
    to serve

GOAN-STYLE SEAFOOD CURRY

Heat the oil in a wok or large skillet over high heat. Add the mustard seeds and stir them around for about 1 minute, or until they jump. Stir in the curry leaves.

Add the shallots and garlic and stir for about 5 minutes, or until the shallots are golden. Stir in the turmeric, coriander, and chili powder and continue stirring for about 30 seconds.

Add the dissolved creamed coconut. Bring to a boil, then reduce the heat to medium and stir for about 2 minutes.

Reduce the heat to low, add the fish, and simmer for 1 minute, spooning the sauce over the fish and very gently stirring it around. Add the shrimp and continue to simmer for an additional 4–5 minutes until the fish flesh flakes easily and the shrimp turn pink and curl.

Add half the lime juice, then taste and add more lime juice and salt to taste. Sprinkle with the lime rind and serve with lime slices.

SERVES 4–6

3 tbsp vegetable oil or peanut oil

1 tbsp black mustard seeds

12 fresh curry leaves or 1 tbsp dried

6 shallots, finely chopped

1 garlic clove, crushed

1 tsp ground turmeric

½ tsp ground coriander

¼–½ tsp chili powder

5 oz/140 g creamed coconut, grated and dissolved in 1¼ cups boiling water

1 lb 2 oz/500 g skinless, boneless white fish, such as monkfish or cod, cut into large chunks

1 lb/450 g large raw shrimp, shelled and deveined

juice and finely grated rind of 1 lime

salt

lime slices, to serve

VEGETABLES

RATATOUILLE

Coarsely chop the eggplants and zucchini, and seed and chop the bell peppers. Slice the onions and finely chop the garlic. Heat the oil in a large skillet. Add the onions and cook over low heat, stirring occasionally, for 5 minutes, or until softened. Add the garlic and cook, stirring frequently for an additional 2 minutes.

Add the eggplants, zucchini, and bell peppers. Increase the heat to medium and cook, stirring occasionally, until the bell peppers begin to color. Add the bouquet garni, reduce the heat, cover, and simmer gently for 40 minutes.

Stir in the chopped tomatoes and season to taste with salt and pepper. Re-cover the pan and simmer gently for an additional 10 minutes. Remove and discard the bouquet garni. Serve warm or cold.

SERVES 4

2 medium-size eggplants

4 zucchini

2 yellow bell peppers

2 red bell peppers

2 onions

2 garlic cloves

$\frac{2}{3}$ cup olive oil

1 bouquet garni

3 large tomatoes, peeled, seeded, and coarsely chopped

salt and pepper

ROAST SUMMER VEGETABLES

Brush an ovenproof dish with a little oil. Arrange the fennel, onions, tomatoes, eggplant, zucchini, and bell peppers in the dish and tuck the garlic cloves and rosemary sprigs among them. Drizzle with the remaining oil and season to taste with pepper.

Roast the vegetables in a preheated oven, 400°F/200°C, for 10 minutes. Turn the vegetables over, return the dish to the oven, and roast for an additional 10–15 minutes or until the vegetables are tender and beginning to turn golden brown.

Serve the vegetables straight from the dish or transfer to a warm serving platter. Serve immediately, with crusty bread, if using, to soak up the juices.

SERVES 4

2 tbsp olive oil

1 fennel bulb, cut into wedges

2 red onions, cut into wedges

2 beefsteak tomatoes, cut into wedges

1 eggplant, thickly sliced

2 zucchini, thickly sliced

1 yellow bell pepper, seeded and cut into chunks

1 red bell pepper, seeded and cut into chunks

1 orange bell pepper, seeded and cut into chunks

4 garlic cloves

4 fresh rosemary sprigs

pepper

crusty bread, to serve (optional)

POTATO & MUSHROOM PIE

Grease a shallow round ovenproof dish with butter.

Layer a quarter of the potatoes in the bottom of the dish. Arrange a quarter of the mushrooms on top of the potatoes and sprinkle with a quarter of the rosemary, chives, and garlic. Continue making layers in the same order, finishing with a layer of potatoes on top.

Pour the heavy cream over the top of the potatoes. Season to taste with salt and pepper.

Cook in a preheated oven, 375°F/190°C, for about 45 minutes or until the pie is golden brown on top and piping hot.

Garnish with snipped chives and serve at once straight from the dish.

SERVES 4

2 tbsp butter

1 lb/450 g waxy potatoes, thinly sliced and parboiled

2 cups sliced mixed mushrooms

1 tbsp chopped rosemary

4 tbsp snipped chives, plus extra to garnish

2 garlic cloves, crushed

²/₃ cup heavy cream

salt and pepper

EGGPLANT GRATIN

Heat the oil in a flameproof casserole over medium heat. Add the onions and cook for 5 minutes or until soft. Add the garlic and cook for a few seconds or until just beginning to color. Using a slotted spoon, transfer the onion mixture to a plate.

Cook the eggplant slices in batches in the same flameproof casserole until they are just lightly browned. Transfer to another plate.

Preheat the oven to 400°F/200°C. Arrange a layer of eggplant slices in the bottom of the casserole dish. Sprinkle with the parsley, thyme, and salt and pepper. Add a layer of onion, tomatoes, and mozzarella, sprinkling parsley, thyme, and salt and pepper over each layer.

Continue layering, finishing with a layer of eggplant slices. Sprinkle with the Parmesan. Bake, uncovered, for 20–30 minutes or until the top is golden and the eggplants are tender. Serve hot.

SERVES 2

4 tbsp olive oil

2 onions, finely chopped

2 garlic cloves, very finely chopped

2 eggplants, thickly sliced

3 tbsp fresh flat-leaf parsley, chopped

½ tsp dried thyme

14 oz/400 g canned chopped tomatoes

1½ cups coarsely grated mozzarella

6 tbsp freshly grated Parmesan

salt and pepper

PARMESAN RISOTTO WITH MUSHROOMS

Heat the oil in a large, deep skillet. Add the rice and cook over low heat, stirring constantly, for 2–3 minutes, until the grains are thoroughly coated in oil and translucent.

Add the garlic, onion, celery, and bell pepper and cook, stirring frequently, for 5 minutes. Add the mushrooms and cook for 3–4 minutes. Stir in the oregano.

Gradually add the hot stock, a ladleful at a time. Stir constantly and add more liquid as the rice absorbs each addition. Increase the heat to medium so that the liquid bubbles. Cook for 20 minutes, or until all the liquid is absorbed and the rice is creamy. Add the sun-dried tomatoes, if using, 5 minutes before the end of the cooking time, then season to taste with salt and pepper.

Remove the risotto from the heat and stir in half the Parmesan until it melts. Transfer the risotto to warmed bowls. Top with the remaining cheese, garnish with flat-leaf parsley or bay leaves, and serve at once.

SERVES 6

2 tbsp olive oil or vegetable oil

generous 1 cup risotto rice

2 garlic cloves, crushed

1 onion, chopped

2 celery stalks, chopped

1 red or green bell pepper, seeded and chopped

8 oz/225 g button mushrooms, thinly sliced

1 tbsp chopped fresh oregano or 1 tsp dried oregano

4 cups boiling vegetable stock

1/4 cup sun-dried tomatoes in olive oil, drained and chopped (optional)

1/2 cup finely grated Parmesan cheese

salt and pepper

fresh flat-leaf parsley sprigs or bay leaves, to garnish

EGG-FRIED RICE WITH VEGETABLES

If you wish to make the crispy onion topping, heat the oil in a large wok or skillet and sauté the onions until crispy and brown. Remove from the pan and keep warm.

To make the rice, heat the oil in a wok or large skillet and sauté the garlic and chiles for 2–3 minutes. Add the mushrooms, snow peas, and corn, and stir-fry for 2–3 minutes before adding the soy sauce, sugar, and basil. Stir in the rice.

Push the mixture to one side of the wok and add the eggs to the bottom. Stir until lightly set before combining into the rice mixture. Serve immediately, topped with the crispy onions if using.

SERVES 4

2 tbsp vegetable oil or peanut oil

2 garlic cloves, finely chopped

2 fresh red chiles, seeded and chopped

4 oz/115 g button mushrooms, sliced

2 oz/55 g snow peas, halved

2 oz/55 g baby corn, halved

3 tbsp Thai soy sauce

1 tbsp light brown sugar

a few Thai basil leaves

3 cups rice, cooked and cooled

2 eggs, beaten

crispy onion topping (optional)

2 tbsp vegetable oil or peanut oil

2 onions, sliced

SPICED
BASMATI PILAU

Place the rice in a strainer and wash well under cold running water. Drain. Trim off most of the broccoli stalk, then quarter the stalk lengthwise and cut diagonally into 1-cm/½-inch pieces. Cut the remaining broccoli into small florets.

Heat the oil in a large skillet. Add the onions and broccoli stalks and cook over low heat, stirring frequently, for 3 minutes. Add the mushrooms, rice, garlic, and spices and cook for 1 minute, stirring, until the rice is coated in oil.

Add the boiling stock and season to taste with salt and pepper. Stir in the broccoli florets and return the mixture to a boil. Cover, reduce the heat, and cook over low heat for 15 minutes without uncovering the pan.

Remove the pan from the heat and let the pilau stand for 5 minutes without uncovering. Remove the whole spices, add the raisins and pistachios, and gently fork through to fluff up the grains. Serve the pilau hot.

SERVES 4

2½ cups basmati rice

6 oz/175 g broccoli, trimmed

6 tbsp vegetable oil

2 large onions, chopped

8 oz/225 g button mushrooms, sliced

2 garlic cloves, crushed

6 cardamom pods, split

6 whole cloves

8 black peppercorns

1 cinnamon stick or piece of cassia bark

1 tsp ground turmeric

5 cups boiling vegetable stock or water

⅓ cup seedless raisins

½ cup unsalted pistachios, coarsely chopped

salt and pepper

MOROCCAN
STEW

Heat the oil in a large, heavy-bottom pan with a tight-fitting lid, and cook the onion, garlic, chile, and eggplant, stirring frequently, for 5–8 minutes, or until softened.

Add the cumin, coriander, and saffron and cook, stirring constantly, for 2 minutes. Bruise the cinnamon stick.

Add the cinnamon, squash, sweet potatoes, prunes, stock, and tomatoes to the pan and bring to a boil. Reduce the heat, then cover and simmer, stirring occasionally, for 20 minutes. Add the chickpeas to the pan and cook for an additional 10 minutes. Discard the cinnamon and serve garnished with the fresh cilantro.

SERVES 4

2 tbsp olive oil

1 red onion, finely chopped

2–4 garlic cloves, crushed

1 fresh red chile, seeded and sliced

1 eggplant, about 8 oz/225 g, cut into small chunks

1 tsp ground cumin

1 tsp ground coriander

pinch of saffron threads

1–2 cinnamon sticks

½–1 butternut squash, about 1 lb/450 g, peeled, seeded, and cut into small chunks

8 oz/225 g sweet potatoes, peeled and cut into small chunks

scant ½ cup prunes

2–2½ cups vegetable stock

4 tomatoes, chopped

14 oz/400 g canned chickpeas, drained and rinsed

1 tbsp chopped fresh cilantro, to garnish

POTATO & LEMON CASSEROLE

Heat the olive oil in a flameproof casserole. Add the onions and sauté over medium heat, stirring frequently, for 3 minutes.

Add the garlic and cook for 30 seconds. Stir in the ground cumin, ground coriander, and cayenne and cook, stirring constantly, for 1 minute.

Add the carrot, turnips, zucchini, and potatoes and stir to coat in the oil.

Add the lemon juice and rind and the vegetable stock. Season to taste with salt and pepper. Cover and cook over medium heat, stirring occasionally, for 20–30 minutes until tender.

Remove the lid, sprinkle in the chopped fresh cilantro and stir well. Serve immediately.

SERVES 4

scant ½ cup olive oil

2 red onions, cut into 8 wedges

3 garlic cloves, crushed

2 tsp ground cumin

2 tsp ground coriander

pinch of cayenne pepper

1 carrot, thickly sliced

2 small turnips, quartered

1 zucchini, sliced

1 lb 2 oz/500 g potatoes, thickly sliced

juice and grated rind of 2 large lemons

1¼ cups vegetable stock

2 tbsp chopped fresh cilantro

salt and pepper

LENTIL & RICE CASSEROLE

Place the lentils, rice, and vegetable stock in a large, flameproof casserole and cook over low heat, stirring occasionally, for 20 minutes.

Add the leek, garlic, tomatoes and their can juice, ground cumin, chili powder, garam masala, sliced bell pepper, broccoli, baby corn, and green beans to the casserole.

Bring the mixture to a boil, reduce the heat, cover, and simmer for an additional 10–15 minutes or until all the vegetables are tender.

Add the shredded basil and season with salt and pepper to taste.

Garnish with fresh basil sprigs and serve immediately.

SERVES 4

1 cup red lentils

generous ¼ cup long-grain rice

5 cups vegetable stock

1 leek, cut into chunks

3 garlic cloves, crushed

14 oz/400 g canned chopped tomatoes

1 tsp ground cumin

1 tsp chili powder

1 tsp garam masala

1 red bell pepper, seeded and sliced

3½ oz/100 g small broccoli florets

8 baby corn, halved lengthwise

2 oz/55 g green beans, halved

1 tbsp shredded fresh basil

salt and pepper

fresh basil sprigs, to garnish

VEGETABLE GOULASH

Put the sun-dried tomatoes in a small heatproof bowl, then cover with almost boiling water and let soak for 15–20 minutes. Drain, reserving the soaking liquid.

Heat the oil in a large, heavy-bottom pan, with a tight-fitting lid, and cook the chiles, garlic, and vegetables, stirring frequently, for 5–8 minutes, or until softened. Blend the tomato paste with a little of the stock in a pitcher and pour over the vegetable mixture, then add the remaining stock, lentils, the sun-dried tomatoes and their soaking liquid, and the paprika.

Bring to a boil, then reduce the heat and simmer, covered, for 15 minutes. Add the fresh tomatoes and simmer for an additional 15 minutes, or until the vegetables and lentils are tender. Serve topped with spoonfuls of sour cream, accompanied by crusty bread.

SERVES 4

¼ cup sun-dried tomatoes, chopped

2 tbsp olive oil

½–1 tsp crushed dried chiles

2–3 garlic cloves, chopped

1 large onion, cut into small wedges

1 small celery root, cut into small chunks

8 oz/225 g carrots, sliced

8 oz/225 g new potatoes, scrubbed and cut into chunks

1 small acorn squash, seeded, peeled, and cut into small chunks, about 8 oz/225 g prepared weight

2 tbsp tomato paste

1¼ cups vegetable stock

2½ cups canned Puy or green lentils, drained and rinsed

1–2 tsp hot paprika

1 lb/450 g ripe tomatoes

sour cream

crusty bread, to serve

RIBOLLITA

Heat the oil in a large saucepan and cook the onions, carrots, and celery for 10–15 minutes, stirring frequently. Add the garlic, thyme, and salt and pepper to taste. Continue to cook for an additional 1–2 minutes, until the vegetables are golden and caramelized.

Add the cannellini beans to the pan and pour in the tomatoes. Add enough of the water to cover the vegetables.

Bring to a boil and simmer for 20 minutes. Add the parsley and Tuscan kale and cook for an additional 5 minutes.

Stir in the bread and add a little more water, if needed. The soup should be thick.

Taste and adjust the seasoning, if needed. Ladle into warmed serving bowls and serve hot, drizzled with extra virgin olive oil.

SERVES 4

3 tbsp olive oil

2 medium red onions, coarsely chopped

3 carrots, sliced

3 celery stalks, coarsely chopped

3 garlic cloves, chopped

1 tbsp chopped fresh thyme

14 oz/400 g canned cannellini beans, drained and rinsed

14 oz/400 g canned chopped tomatoes

2½ cups water or vegetable stock

2 tbsp chopped fresh parsley

1 lb 2 oz/500 g Tuscan kale or Savoy cabbage, trimmed and sliced

1 small day-old ciabatta loaf, torn into small pieces

salt and pepper

extra virgin olive oil, to serve

TUSCAN BEAN
STEW

Trim the fennel and reserve any feathery fronds, then cut the bulb into small strips. Heat the oil in a large, heavy-bottom pan with a tight-fitting lid, and cook the onion, garlic, chile, and fennel strips, stirring frequently, for 5–8 minutes, or until softened.

Add the eggplant and cook, stirring frequently, for 5 minutes. Blend the tomato paste with a little of the stock in a pitcher and pour over the fennel mixture, then add the remaining stock, and the tomatoes, vinegar, and oregano. Bring to a boil, then reduce the heat and simmer, covered, for 15 minutes, or until the tomatoes have begun to collapse.

Drain and rinse the beans, then drain again. Add them to the pan with the yellow bell pepper, zucchini, and olives. Simmer for an additional 15 minutes, or until the vegetables are tender. Taste and adjust the seasoning. Scatter with the Parmesan shavings and serve garnished with the reserved fennel fronds, accompanied by polenta wedges or crusty bread.

SERVES 4

1 large fennel bulb

2 tbsp olive oil

1 red onion, cut into small wedges

2–4 garlic cloves, sliced

1 fresh green chile, seeded
   and chopped

1 small eggplant, about
   8 oz/225 g, cut into chunks

2 tbsp tomato paste

scant 2–2½ cups vegetable stock

1 lb/450 g ripe tomatoes

1 tbsp balsamic vinegar

a few sprigs of fresh oregano

14 oz/400 g canned borlotti beans

14 oz/400 g canned flageolets

1 yellow bell pepper, seeded and
   cut into small strips

1 zucchini, sliced into half moons

⅓ cup pitted black olives

1 oz/25 g Parmesan cheese,
   freshly shaved

salt and pepper

polenta wedges or crusty bread,
   to serve

KIDNEY BEAN, PUMPKIN & TOMATO STEW

Pick over the beans, cover generously with cold water, and set aside to soak for 6 hours or overnight. Drain the beans, put in a large saucepan, and add enough cold water to cover by 2 inches. Bring to a boil and simmer for 10 minutes. Drain and rinse well. Clean the saucepan.

Heat the oil in the cleaned saucepan over medium heat. Add the onions, cover, and cook for 3–4 minutes, until they are just softened, stirring occasionally. Add the garlic, celery, and carrot, and continue cooking for 2 minutes.

Add the water, drained beans, tomato paste, thyme, oregano, cumin, and bay leaf. When the mixture begins to bubble, reduce the heat to low. Cover and simmer gently for 1 hour, stirring occasionally.

Stir in the tomatoes, pumpkin, and chili paste and continue simmering for an additional hour, or until the beans and pumpkin are tender, stirring from time to time.

Season to taste with salt and pepper and stir in a little more chili paste, if desired. Remove the bay leaf. Ladle the soup into bowls, garnish with cilantro, and serve.

SERVES 4–6

9 oz/250 g dried kidney beans

1 tbsp olive oil

2 onions, finely chopped

4 garlic cloves, finely chopped

1 celery stalk, thinly sliced

1 carrot, halved and thinly sliced

5 cups water

2 tsp tomato paste

⅛ tsp dried thyme

⅛ tsp dried oregano

⅛ tsp ground cumin

1 bay leaf

14 oz/400 g canned chopped tomatoes

9 oz/250 g peeled pumpkin flesh, diced

¼ tsp chili paste, or to taste

salt and pepper

fresh cilantro, to garnish

DESSERTS

APPLE & BLACKBERRY CRUMBLE

Preheat the oven to 400°F/200°C.

Peel and core the apples and cut into chunks. Place in a bowl with the blackberries, sugar, and cinnamon and mix together, then transfer to an ovenproof baking dish.

To make the crumble topping, sift the self-rising flour into a bowl and stir in the whole wheat flour. Add the butter and rub it in with your fingertips until the mixture resembles fine breadcrumbs. Stir in the sugar.

Spread the crumble over the fruit and bake in the preheated oven for 40–45 minutes, or until the apples are soft and the crumble is golden brown and crisp. Serve with cream.

DESSERTS

162

SERVES 4

2 lb/900 g tart cooking apples, peeled and sliced

10½ oz/300 g blackberries, fresh or frozen

¼ cup brown sugar

1 tsp ground cinnamon

crumble topping
⅔ cup self-rising flour

⅔ cup whole wheat flour

½ cup unsalted butter

¼ cup raw brown sugar

RHUBARB CRUMBLE

Preheat the oven to 375°F/190°C.

Cut the rhubarb into 1-inch/2.5-cm lengths and put in an ovenproof dish with the superfine sugar and the orange rind and juice.

To make the crumble topping, sift the flour into a bowl. Rub in the butter with your fingertips until the mixture resembles fine breadcrumbs. Stir in the brown sugar and ginger. Spread evenly over the fruit and press down lightly with a fork.

Bake in the center of the preheated oven for 25–30 minutes until the crumble is golden brown.

Serve warm with cream, yogurt, or custard.

SERVES 6

2 lb/900 g rhubarb

½ cup superfine sugar

grated rind and juice of 1 orange

cream, yogurt, or custard, to serve

crumble topping

scant 1⅝ cups all-purpose or
    whole wheat flour

½ cup unsalted butter, diced and
    chilled

½ cup light brown sugar

1 tsp ground ginger

APRICOT
CRUMBLE

Preheat the oven to 400°F/200°C.

Put 3 tablespoons of the butter and ¾ cup of the sugar in a saucepan and melt together, stirring, over low heat. Add the apricots and cinnamon, cover the saucepan, and simmer for 5 minutes.

To make the crumble topping, put the flour in a bowl and rub in the remaining butter with your fingertips until the mixture resembles fine breadcrumbs. Stir in the remaining sugar and then the hazelnuts.

Remove the fruit from the heat and arrange in the bottom of an ovenproof dish. Sprinkle the crumble topping evenly over the fruit until it is covered all over. Transfer to the preheated oven and bake for about 25 minutes, until golden. Remove from the oven and serve hot with cream.

SERVES 6

generous ½ cup unsalted butter, plus extra for greasing

1 cup brown sugar

3 cups pitted and sliced fresh apricots

1 tsp ground cinnamon

light or heavy cream, to serve

crumble topping

1½ cups whole wheat flour

½ cup hazelnuts, toasted and finely chopped

SHERRIED NECTARINE DESSERT

Preheat the oven to 400°F/200°C.

Using a sharp knife, halve the nectarines, remove and discard the pits, then cut the flesh into fairly thick slices. Put the nectarine slices into an ovenproof dish, sprinkle over the sugar and sweet sherry, then cook in the preheated oven for 5–10 minutes until heated through.

To make the crumble topping, put the flour and sugar in a large bowl, then quickly mix in the melted butter until crumbly. Carefully arrange the crumble over the nectarines in an even layer—keep your touch light or the crumble will sink into the filling and get mushy. Scatter a little more sugar over the top, then transfer to the preheated oven and bake for 25–30 minutes or until the crumble topping is golden brown.

Remove from the oven and serve with generous spoonfuls of cream.

SERVES 4

6 nectarines

1 oz/25 g raw brown sugar

2 tbsp sweet sherry

light or heavy cream, to serve

crumble topping

1¼ cups all-purpose flour

¼ cup raw brown sugar, plus extra for sprinkling

½ cup unsalted butter, melted

GOOSEBERRY & PISTACHIO DESSERT

Preheat the oven to 400°F/200°C.

Put the gooseberries in an ovenproof dish, pour over the honey, and cook in the preheated oven for 5–10 minutes until heated through.

Put the superfine sugar, orange juice, orange zest, and water in a small saucepan, then bring to a boil, stirring, over medium heat. Reduce the heat and simmer for 5 minutes, then remove from the heat and set aside to cool.

Meanwhile, to make the crumble topping, put the flour in a bowl, then rub in the butter with your fingertips until the mixture resembles fine breadcrumbs. Now stir in 4 tablespoons of the raw brown sugar and the pistachios.

Pour the cooled orange syrup over the gooseberries, then lightly sprinkle over the crumble mixture in an even layer. Do not press the crumble into the syrup or it will become mushy. Sprinkle over the remaining raw brown sugar.

Bake in the preheated oven for 25–30 minutes or until the crumble topping is golden brown. Remove from the oven and serve with crème fraîche.

DESSERTS

170

SERVES 4

14 oz/400 g gooseberries

1 tbsp honey

½ cup superfine sugar

1 tbsp orange juice

1 tbsp grated orange zest

6 tbsp water

crème fraîche

crumble topping

¾ cup self-rising flour

½ cup unsalted butter, diced

5 tbsp raw brown sugar

1¾ oz/50 g pistachios, finely chopped

FRUIT COBBLER

Preheat the oven to 400°F/200°C.

Pick over the fruit, then mix with the superfine sugar and cornstarch and put in a 10-inch/25-cm shallow, ovenproof dish.

To make the cobbler topping, sift the flour, baking powder, and salt into a large bowl. Rub in the butter with your fingertips until the mixture resembles fine breadcrumbs, then stir in the superfine sugar. Pour in the buttermilk and mix to a soft dough.

Drop spoonfuls of the dough on top of the fruit roughly, so that it doesn't completely cover the fruit. Sprinkle with the raw brown sugar and bake in the preheated oven for 25–30 minutes, or until the crust is golden and the fruit is tender.

Remove from the oven and set aside for a few minutes before serving.

SERVES 6

2 lb/900 g fresh berries and currants, such as blackberries, blueberries, raspberries, red currants, and black currants

½ cup superfine sugar

2 tbsp cornstarch

cobbler topping

1⅓ cups all-purpose flour

2 tsp baking powder

pinch of salt

4 tbsp unsalted butter, diced and chilled

2 tbsp superfine sugar

¾ cup buttermilk

1 tbsp raw brown sugar

STRAWBERRY CREAM COBBLER

Preheat the oven to 400°F/200°C.

Arrange the strawberries evenly in the bottom of an ovenproof dish, then sprinkle over the sugar and cook in the preheated oven for 5–10 minutes until heated through.

To make the cobbler topping, sift the flour and salt into a large mixing bowl. Rub in the butter with your fingertips until the mixture resembles fine breadcrumbs, then stir in the sugar. Add the beaten egg, then the golden raisins and raisins and mix lightly until incorporated. Stir in enough of the milk to make a smooth dough. Transfer to a clean, lightly floured board, knead lightly, then roll out to a thickness of about ½ inch/1 cm. Cut out circles using a 2-inch/5-cm cookie cutter. Arrange the dough circles over the strawberries, then brush the tops with a little milk.

Bake in the preheated oven for 25–30 minutes, or until the cobbler topping has risen and is lightly golden. Remove from the oven and serve with whipped heavy cream.

SERVES 4

1 lb 12 oz/800 g strawberries, hulled and halved

¼ cup superfine sugar

whipped heavy cream, to serve

cobbler topping

1½ cups self-rising flour, plus extra for dusting

pinch of salt

3 tbsp unsalted butter

2 tbsp superfine sugar

1 egg, beaten

1 oz/25 g golden raisins

1 oz/25 g raisins

5 tbsp milk, plus extra for glazing

SPICED MANGO & BLUEBERRY COBBLER

Preheat the oven to 400°F/200°C.

Put the mangoes and blueberries in the bottom of an ovenproof saucepan, then sprinkle over the nutmeg, lime juice, and superfine sugar and cook in the preheated oven for 5–10 minutes until heated through.

To make the cobbler topping, sift the flour, salt, and cinnamon into a large mixing bowl. Rub in the butter with your fingertips until the mixture resembles fine breadcrumbs, then mix in the sugar and the dried blueberries, if using. Add the beaten egg, then stir in enough of the milk to make a smooth dough. Transfer to a clean, lightly floured board, knead lightly, then roll out to a thickness of about ½ inch/1 cm. Cut out circles using a 2-inch/5-cm cookie cutter. Arrange the dough circles over the fruit, then brush the tops with a little milk.

Bake in the preheated oven for 25–30 minutes, or until the cobbler topping has risen and is lightly golden. Remove from the oven and serve.

SERVES 4

2 ripe mangoes, pitted and cut into fairly thick slices

9 oz/250 g blueberries

½ tsp grated nutmeg

1 tbsp lime juice

¼ cup superfine sugar, or to taste

cobbler topping

1½ cups self-rising flour, plus extra for dusting

pinch of salt

½ tsp cinnamon

3 tbsp unsalted butter

2 tbsp superfine sugar

3 tbsp dried blueberries (optional)

1 egg, beaten

5 tbsp milk, plus extra for glazing

CHOCOLATE BROWNIES

Preheat the oven to 350°F/180°C. Grease and line an 11 x 7-inch/ 28 x 18-cm rectangular cake pan with parchment paper.

Put the butter and chopped dark chocolate into a heatproof bowl and set over a saucepan of simmering water until melted. Remove from the heat. Sift the flour into a large bowl, add the sugar, and mix well. Stir the eggs into the chocolate mixture then beat into the flour mixture. Add the nuts, golden raisins, and chocolate chips, and mix well. Spoon evenly into the cake pan and level the surface.

Bake in the oven for 30 minutes, or until firm. To check whether the cake is cooked through, insert a skewer into the center—it should come out clean. If not, return the cake to the oven for a few minutes. Remove from the oven and let cool for 15 minutes. Turn out onto a wire rack to cool completely. To decorate, drizzle the melted white chocolate in fine lines over the cake, then cut into bars or squares. Set aside to set before serving.

MAKES 15

8 oz/225 g unsalted butter, diced, plus extra for greasing

5½ oz/150 g dark chocolate, chopped

1½ cups all-purpose flour

1 cup dark brown sugar

4 eggs, beaten

¼ cup chopped blanched hazelnuts

½ cup golden raisins

½ cup dark chocolate chips

4 oz/115 g white chocolate, melted, to decorate

UPSIDE-DOWN TOFFEE APPLE BROWNIES

Preheat the oven to 350°F/180°C. Grease a 9-inch/23-cm square shallow cake pan.

For the topping, place the sugar and remaining butter in a small saucepan and heat gently, stirring, until melted. Pour into the prepared cake pan. Arrange the apple slices on top.

For the brownies, place the butter and sugar in a bowl and beat well until pale and fluffy. Gradually beat in the eggs.

Sift together the flour, baking powder, baking soda, and spice and fold into the mixture. Stir in the apples and nuts.

Pour into the prepared cake pan and bake for 35–40 minutes until firm and golden. Cool in the pan for 10 minutes, then turn out upside down and cut into squares.

MAKES 9

toffee apple topping

generous ⅓ cup light brown sugar

2 oz/55 g unsalted butter, plus extra for greasing

1 apple, cored and thinly sliced

brownies

4 oz/115 g unsalted butter

¾ cup light brown sugar

2 eggs, beaten

1¾ cups all-purpose flour

1 tsp baking powder

½ tsp baking soda

1½ tsp apple pie spice

2 apples, peeled and coarsely grated

¾ cup chopped hazelnuts

CHOCOLATE MARSHMALLOW FINGERS

Put the graham crackers in a plastic bag and, using a rolling pin, crush into small pieces.

Put the chocolate, butter, sugar, cocoa, and honey in a saucepan and heat gently until melted. Remove from the heat and cool slightly.

Stir the crushed crackers into the chocolate mixture until well mixed. Add the marshmallows and mix well then finally stir in the chocolate chips.

Turn the mixture into an 8-inch/20-cm square cake pan and lightly smooth the top. Put in the refrigerator and let chill for 2–3 hours until set. Cut into fingers before serving.

MAKES 18

12 oz/350 g graham crackers

4½ oz/125 g semisweet chocolate, broken into pieces

8 oz/225 g unsalted butter

2 tbsp superfine sugar

2 tbsp unsweetened cocoa

2 tbsp honey

⅔ cup mini marshmallows

½ cup white chocolate chips

RICH VANILLA
ICE CREAM

Pour the light and heavy cream into a large, heavy-bottom saucepan. Split open the vanilla bean and scrape out the seeds into the cream, then add the whole vanilla bean. Bring almost to a boil, then remove from the heat and set aside for 30 minutes.

Put the egg yolks and sugar in a large bowl and whisk together until pale and the mixture leaves a trail when the whisk is lifted. Remove the vanilla bean from the cream, then slowly add the cream to the egg mixture, stirring all the time with a wooden spoon. Strain the mixture into the rinsed-out saucepan and cook over low heat for 10–15 minutes, stirring all the time, until the mixture thickens enough to coat the back of the spoon. Do not let the mixture boil or it will curdle. Remove the custard from the heat and cool for at least 1 hour, stirring from time to time to prevent a skin from forming.

If using an ice-cream machine, churn the cold custard in the machine following the manufacturer's instructions. Alternatively, freeze the custard in a freezerproof container, uncovered, for 1–2 hours or until it starts to set around the edges. Turn the custard into a bowl and stir with a fork or beat in a food processor until smooth. Return to the freezer and freeze for an additional 2–3 hours, or until firm or ready to serve. Cover the container with a lid for storing.

SERVES 4–6

1¼ cups light cream and
    1¼ cups heavy cream

1 vanilla bean

4 large egg yolks

generous ½ cup superfine sugar

CHOCOLATE
ICE CREAM

Pour the milk into a large, heavy-bottom saucepan. Split open the vanilla bean and scrape out the seeds into the milk, then add the whole vanilla bean. Bring almost to a boil, then remove from the heat and set aside for 30 minutes. Remove the vanilla bean from the milk. Break the chocolate into the milk and heat gently, stirring constantly, until melted and smooth.

Put the egg yolks and sugar in a large bowl and whisk together until pale and the mixture leaves a trail when the whisk is lifted. Gradually add the chocolate mixture, stirring constantly with a wooden spoon. Strain the mixture into the rinsed-out saucepan and cook over low heat for 10–15 minutes, stirring constantly, until the mixture thickens enough to coat the back of a wooden spoon. Do not let the mixture boil or it will curdle. Remove the custard from the heat and let cool for at least 1 hour, stirring occasionally to prevent a skin from forming. Meanwhile, whip the cream until it holds its shape. Set aside in the refrigerator until ready to use.

If using an ice-cream machine, fold the whipped cream into the cold custard, then churn the mixture in the machine following the manufacturer's instructions. Alternatively, freeze the custard in a freezerproof container, uncovered, for 1–2 hours or until it begins to set around the edges. Turn the custard into a bowl and stir with a fork or beat in a food processor until smooth. Fold in the whipped cream. Return to the freezer and freeze for 2–3 hours more, or until firm or ready to serve. Cover the container with a lid for storing.

SERVES 4–6

1¼ cups milk

1 vanilla bean

3½ oz/100 g semisweet chocolate

3 egg yolks

scant ½ cup superfine sugar

1¼ cups heavy cream

HONEYCOMB ICE CREAM

Grease a baking sheet with butter. Put the sugar and syrup in a heavy-bottom saucepan and heat gently until the sugar melts. Boil for 1–2 minutes, or until beginning to caramelize, being careful not to let the mixture burn. Stir in the baking soda, then immediately pour the mixture onto the prepared baking sheet but do not spread. Set aside to stand for about 10 minutes, until cold.

When the honeycomb is cold, put it into a strong plastic bag and crush into small pieces using a rolling pin or meat mallet. Whip the cream until it holds its shape, then whisk in the condensed milk.

If using an ice-cream machine, churn the mixture in the machine following the manufacturer's instructions. Just before the ice cream freezes, add the honeycomb pieces. Alternatively, freeze the custard in a freezerproof container, uncovered, for 1–2 hours or until it begins to set around the edges. Turn the custard into a bowl and stir with a fork or beat in a food processor until smooth. Fold in the honeycomb pieces. Return to the freezer and freeze for 2–3 hours more, or until firm or ready to serve. Cover the container with a lid for storing.

SERVES 6–8

unsalted butter, for greasing

scant ½ cup granulated sugar

2 tbsp light corn syrup

1 tsp baking soda

1¾ cups heavy cream

14 oz/400 g canned
   condensed milk

INDEX